Before The Dawn:
A Night of Memories

Mary Lu Warstler

Rodneyjw @ 1st. net

PublishAmerica
Baltimore

ISBN: 1-59129-438-X
PUBLISHED BY PUBLISHAMERICA BOOK
PUBLISHERS
www.publishamerica.com
Baltimore

Printed in the United States of America

DEDICATION

To Rodney for his patience with me
while I spent hours at the computer
and
To all my friends at
Kenmore United Methodist Church
who have encouraged me in writing this book.

A WORD OF THANKS

I need to say a word of thanks to many people for their help in constructing and writing this story. When I first began writing it in the form of monologues, and later added characters to give it more life and meaning, the folks at Kenmore United Methodist Church in Akron, Ohio, were there to support and encourage me all the way, especially the Seekers Sunday School Class and the Mary Circle of the United Methodist Women. Reverend Rolland and Martha Reece went the second mile in reading, commenting, and giving me ideas and help for many changes and improvements which were made.

When I first began to think in terms of a book, I was in seminary. One of my professors, Sister Joanmarie Smith, gave me many words of encouragement.

I asked my friend, Dr. Ted Mayer, who was a retired United Methodist Pastor and former District Superintendent, to read the first drafts. He was thrilled to do so, and without his encouragement, I may not have proceeded any further. Dr. Mayer has since gone to his eternal reward, but his memory helped me along the way.

Alberta Hawse, author and friend, invited me to join a writer's group at her home. She has encouraged me, criticized me, complimented me, and given me hope. She has truly been a friend. Without her help, it would have been more difficult to stay the course and finish the task. Friends in the group, Sylvia, Gay, and Kathryn all have been a great help in keeping me at the task with encouraging words and critical comments as we sought to help each other.

When I was appointed to the First United Methodist Church in Bucyrus, Ohio, I continued to find support and encouragement from the folks in the church and even in the community. I am especially grateful to Martha Ann Lown for her long and diligent reading and re-reading of the manuscript, offering her expertise in English and understanding of story as a vehicle of expressing our faith. I can never find enough words to express the help she has given.

My family has been supportive and encouraging since I first started writing. Many times I took their advice and comments with a grain of salt. After all, family is supposed to praise your work. But they more often than not had good critical comments and I tried to take them to heart.

I need to say a special thank you to all who read a great number of drafts, re-writes, and edit forms of this manuscript.

It has been a joy working with so many. It has been even more of a joy discovering the story within the story.

Table of Contents

INTRODUCTION

From the moment of conception – and before – Jesus' life was destined for Golgotha. It was not until after his baptism, however, that he resolutely set his footsteps toward Jerusalem, Golgotha, and the cross – his ultimate goal. Because he was human, he must have struggled as he grew in stature, waiting for the right time to begin his ministry. Because he was God incarnate, he must have been frustrated with his human limitations. Could any of us ever guess what it would be like to be the Son of God, full of power and yet limited by human flesh? In a power-filled world where wealth is most important, why would anyone choose to be a servant? But Jesus did just that.

On his journey to the cross, which took approximately two and a half to three years, Jesus met more than just the few folks named in our Scripture. Lives were changed when people met him and believed him to be the Christ. It would have been impossible for the writers of the Gospels to make a complete and thorough biography of his life. Their intent was simply to give their readers enough stories to reassure faith in order that the Word of God might be spread.

As a pastor and Bible teacher, I often heard questions concerning the difficulty of connecting the Scriptures with the here and now. Life in the Twentieth Century, and now in the Twenty-first Century, is different from the days of Jesus. Some see Jesus as so superior to humans that neither we can understand him, nor he can understand us.

I believe people who knew Jesus personally were much like people of all generations. Some lived with poverty and struggle. Many lived rough lives that would probably be frowned upon by decent folks, both in their day and in ours. But Jesus, who lived among the people, knew all kinds of folks and loved them anyway.

In this work of fiction I have tried to portray some people whose lives intersected with Jesus' life. While much of the material is fact, I have filled in gaps with what could have been. I see each character as a real person who, after meeting Jesus, saw life differently. Hope became real even in the dark hours of Golgotha. In the last hours before dawn of the first day of the week – the third day after the crucifixion – stories are shared with the hope of encouraging one another and keeping memories of Jesus alive.

Although this is not meant to be an accurate, scholarly exegesis, nor even a theological account, there are some elements of both within the pages of these few chapters. I have faithfully tried to adhere to the truths of the Scripture, but have also let my imagination run free in expressing what could have been. It is simply one way of looking at life today compared with the lives of men, women and children who were changed by following the road to Jerusalem with Jesus.

Throughout this book I offer footnotes as reference guides only. They are not direct quotes, but only a help in finding the story as told in our Scriptures. They are found at the end of the book.

People of all centuries have known grief – a complex emotion. Tears flow one minute, and words of anger come unbidden the next. Even laughter, as inappropriate as it seems, is a part of the total mix of grief. Often the best therapy for grief is time with friends, each expressing memories.

Family and friends who were closest to Jesus were disappointed, frustrated, and grief-stricken by his untimely and violent death. Their plans had become useless and they were confused about what to do next. They feared for their own safety, but needed to be together as they grieved the loss of their friend and Master.

Having experienced grief in my own life, and that of many parishioners, I know how death affects the lives of loved ones. It has been no different throughout history. The death of Jesus affected people of his day much the same as it does people of all generations. When we begin to understand his relationship with the people then, we can better understand how he touches the lives of people in all times. More importantly, we can begin to see how he works within each of our own lives.

Old clichés like "night is darkest before the dawn" take on new meaning when death touches our lives – especially as we wait those final hours before the last goodbye. It certainly did for those men, women and young folks who had gathered for shared comfort in Jerusalem. Questions concerning the events of the preceding days filled the conversations as they waited for the dawn of a new day which would probably bring more questions. *BEFORE THE DAWN: A Night of Memories* expresses some of those questions. Memories are shared, along with shattered hopes and dreams. Together the few followers struggle with hope for the future.

My hope and dream for this book are two-fold: (1) I hope the reader will begin to see similarities between life as it was when Jesus was here on earth, and life as we know it to be in our own century. Then we can begin to find strength and hope for our own dark nights, looking toward a new day of dawn and miracles with renewed hope. And (2) I hope the reader will be encouraged to look beyond the facts of the Scripture to the way God works in our lives in our own everyday world.

BEFORE THE DAWN: A Night of Memories is an attempt to reveal some memories and feelings which we all embrace in times of grief. With mingled joy and sadness we remember shared events of the past. We often wish it had been different – that we had said and done things to show our love. It was no different for the friends of Jesus. We know how the story ends because we read it from the perspective of distance. Therefore, we know what the friends gathered that night before the Third Day did not know.

The story begins to unfold in the prologue as we follow Simon Peter when the disciples leave the Upper Room for the Garden of Gethsemane. It continues as many folks gather in John's house and settle in for the long night before the Third Day.

Prologue

A Night of Betrayal

Bright, twinkling stars competed with the full moon, showing off their brilliance. A slight breeze played with the palm leaves as crickets chirped their night song under the trees. Had anyone been tracking the beauty of nights, this one would be close in splendor to that one thirty-some years earlier in a little town called Bethlehem, when an infant's cry split the night's silence. That child, now grown, would weep once again this night, but his cries would be silent and his tears flow like drops of crimson blood.

Crickets fell silent as Jesus and his disciples filed out of the home where they completed the Passover meal in the upper room. As was his custom, Jesus turned toward Olivet to pray.[1] The disciples followed, with less enthusiasm. Even though they were excited, they were also physically tired.

Simon Peter paused to gaze at the stars. He was too keyed up for his thoughts to make much sense, but nothing could take away his excitement. The Messiah would soon set up his kingdom. If only he could rid himself of that feeling of foreboding which nipped at the edges of his thoughts like an uncontrolled mongrel.

The night breeze, tired of its game with the leaves, brushed against his wispy hair, teasing it into more tangles. Peter pulled thoughtfully at his beard. *Why did Judas leave before the rest of us? Where did he go? Will he be at Olivet later?* Combing his fingers through his hair, Peter sought unsuccessfully to comb away his tangled thoughts. It would be futile to worry about Judas, who was always a step or two out of sync with the others anyway. Why Jesus ever chose him over his friend Lazarus, he would never understand. And why did he give Judas charge of the money bag instead Matthew, who was better qualified and more experienced? Peter didn't intend to linger, but got lost in his inner turmoil. He didn't even notice the others moving on without him.

"Hey, Peter! Are you coming with us or not?" John's urgent call pulled him from his troublesome thoughts. The breeze, which continued to mockingly caress his face and tug at his hair, sent a chill down his spine. Somewhere in the distance a dog yapped noisily in the otherwise calm night. Peter's fisherman instinct lifted his eyes skyward, looking for an approaching storm, or some reason for his uneasy feeling. Only the stars and moon filled the sky.

Giving himself a mental shake that spilled into a physical shiver, Peter answered, "I'm coming." He ran to catch the others, hoping they wouldn't notice him gasping for air as he caught up to them.

"What were you doing?" Andrew poked his finger in his brother's ribs. "Daydreaming?"

"Maybe he was planning his acceptance speech as the Director of the King's Cabinet," laughed Philip.

Andrew laughed boisterously and the rest joined him. Peter didn't think it was so funny and glanced toward Jesus, hoping he had not heard. Jesus seemed too preoccupied to make any comment. With a sigh of relief, Peter trailed along a step or two behind the rest. *Jesus must have a lot of planning to do,* he thought. *We would help him if he would just tell us what needs to be done.*

Steps which started as excited skips and hops began to wane to a slow dance of weariness. How easy it would have been to fall into a leisurely stroll. However, as they neared Olivet, Jesus picked up the pace, almost jogging along. His Disciples had to run just to keep up with him. Peter sensed urgency in the Master. *I wonder if he's getting nervous about the coming kingdom,* he thought.

Soon they were trudging wearily up the Mount of Olives. One by one, the disciples dropped to the ground, panting for breath. They knew they were expected to pray. Judas knew the place and would have no trouble finding them later – if he bothered to come at all. He probably went home to get some rest before tomorrow. Peter was disgusted with Judas.

So many times they had prayed with Jesus in that garden on Mount Olivet, they were not surprised when Jesus moved toward a boulder in a small clearing. He often used it to rest his arms and head upon when he prayed. Nor were they surprised when he called, "Peter, James and John, come with me. My soul is heavy and I need companionship."[2]

Weary as he was, Peter jumped up and ran after Jesus. When Jesus wanted the three of them, it was urgent. James and John also pulled themselves to their feet and followed.

"Stay here and pray with me." Jesus pointed out another small area naked of shrubbery. "I will go over to that boulder and pray. Please, my soul is so heavy. Pray with me." At the boulder Jesus dropped to his knees, as if the weight of the world rested upon his shoulders, pulling him down. His head fell heavily on his arms as he hugged the top of the stone.

Peter, James and John dropped wearily to the ground. Pushing aside a branch here and a stone there and smoothing a spot for his body, John soon fell into his prayer. James also brushed aside branches, pebbles and bugs and began to pray. Peter struggled with the sticks and stones. He moved this way and that until finally he was in relative comfort. Not certain what he should be doing, he began to pray, asking God's will for whatever would come. Remembering Jesus' words to pray for courage in the hour of trial, he prayed that Jesus was wrong about him betraying him. A few clouds drifted across the sky, cutting the little trickle of light to only a flicker here and there.

Peter couldn't understand why the feeling of impending doom still nagged at him, when everything seemed quiet and peaceful. He glanced at James and John, wondering if they felt the way he did. Even though they were brothers, they were different. He had seen James, the younger of the two, haul in large nets of fish with his brother, but he knew James' heart was never in fishing. Fishing was too tame. James needed more action.

John, however, was more easygoing. He loved fishing and would still be with his father if Jesus hadn't said, "Come follow me." John would always be loyal and true.

And then there is me, Simon Peter. He shifted positions, rubbing the tender flesh of his hips where a small twig was jabbing him. *I always seem to put my foot in my mouth. I'm too easily riled and have a quick temper, but I'm strong enough to pull in a net of fish with little effort.*

Peter was beginning to feel self-confident and proud. Suddenly he remembered the purpose was to pray. With a smirk, he noticed James and John beginning to nod, not even noticing the weightlessness of his own body. Darkness, the warmth of his coat pulled tightly around him, and the long day soon weighed heavily on his blinking eyelids. Peter became the third in a trio of snores.

Meanwhile, Jesus prayed at his altar. His heart became so heavy he thought it would break. Sighing heavily, he wondered if Peter, James and John were as heavy-hearted as he. Anchored to the boulder like a magnet, Jesus had to force himself away from his kneeling position. He trudged heavily to his praying friends. Their snores belied their promise to pray.

Gently Jesus shook them each in turn. "You need to pray. The night gets shorter. The time draws near." His words were short and urgent. Time was running out. He returned to his altar.

Shamefaced, the three friends shook themselves, got up and walked around the tiny little clearing, then settled once more. They tried to pray, but as before, eyes began to feel like lead, and chins soon rested on chests heaving rhythmically in sleep.

When Jesus returned a second time, a little anger, frustration, fear – not for himself, but for them – gave an edge to his words. "Wake up. Don't you realize the danger?"

"Danger? What danger?" Peter jumped groggily to his feet, trying to draw his sword in the process. It was awkward. He was a fisherman, not a swordsman. He only bought it so he would be prepared for the coming Kingdom. Wildly waving the long, broad blade around, he looked for the danger.

"Put that thing away before you hurt someone," shouted John. James jumping to his feet, tripped over John. Together they tumbled in a heap before Jesus. Jesus smiled in spite of his anguish. These men his Father gave him were just too much sometimes. They tried so hard, but they were so human.

"Please pray," he gently chided them and returned to his own anguishing prayers. Even in the cold night breeze, sweat poured from his brow as from an open wound. Soon he heard the familiar sounds of the three snores all keeping a peculiar rhythm of peace.

"Father, they are mine. Keep them safe. Now, if this cup cannot pass from me, then let your complete will be done." As the angels sang so long ago, peace on earth was accomplished – but not a peace without pain.

Far down the hill near the garden gate, tiny specks of blinking lights staggered upward, nearing to the place where Jesus and his disciples prayed. Sounds of many feet crunching on the stones sent a warning to the other sleeping disciples. Startled, they woke and saw Judas in the light of the torch he carried. He must be bringing help for the kingdom, they thought.[3]

"Where's Jesus?" Judas swaggered closer to them. His voice had a strange, almost hysterical ring to it. An alarm sounded in the foggy, sleep-drugged minds too late. The crowd was a mob, not an organized group of helpers. Still, why was Judas was with them? Instinctively they closed ranks to the pathway to Jesus.

Jesus roused his three sleeping friends again, a different sound of urgency in his voice. "Wake up. The time has come. My betrayer is here."

Minds still sluggish with sleep, the bodies jumped to attention. "Betrayer? What betrayer?" Peter once again drew his sword and began swinging it. His eyes fell on Judas and he stopped mid-swing, the heavy sword almost pulling him over.

Judas rushed to Jesus and kissed him in greeting. "Sorry I'm late, Master, but you know how it is." Having received their signal, the mob moved to take Jesus captive.

It only took seconds for Peter and the others to feel the impact of that kiss. Temple guards stepped forward with ropes. People shouted. Chaos reigned. Nothing made sense. Peter watched the servant of the High Priest strike Jesus. Muscles unfroze, allowing his sword to fall with a crashing blow and the servant's ear fell to the ground. Peter raised his sword, blood dripping from its edge, to finish the job.

Jesus' stern words filled him with confusion. "Stop! It is enough. There will be no killing."

Peter watched in shock – mouth open, eyes wide, sword still held above his head – as Jesus picked up the fallen ear and replaced it on the man's head. It was as if the sword had never touched him. Jesus left without struggle, led by Judas and the mob. Disbelief rendered the disciples mute.

Someone shouted, "Get the followers, too. Let's get rid of all of them at once." Laughter followed and a few turned back to take more captives. Without a word the disciples began to scatter. Peter slowly lowered his sword, staring at it, trying to focus. What was the strange thing in his hand? Recognition dawned and his stare turned to a look of horror. The sword seemed to have come to life, ready to strike like a serpent. He hurled the evil thing as far from him as his strength would allow. Finally his paralyzed throat muscles allowed sound to spew forth as he ran. "No! No!" Only moments before that garden had been a place of quiet prayer.

Peter could not move fast enough. Tripping in his haste, he fell to his knees and began crawling toward the path where he pulled himself up by a low-hanging tree branch. He had to follow Jesus. He would stay far enough back not to be seen, but close enough to hear.[4] Painful as it was, he had to know what was happening. Surely this was all a dream. Soon he would wake and find Jesus still praying. The cool breeze had turned cold. It whipped around him, telling him he was not dreaming.

The mob pushed Judas aside and took Jesus to Pilate. Peter stepped into the shadows of the courtyard, where guards and a few servants milled around, eager for the latest gossip. A charcoal fire burned brightly in the center of the yard. Peter shivered violently – probably not from the chill of the night. He hoped to get close enough for the warmth to stop his trembling.

Maybe no one will know me, he thought as he reached his hands toward the heat. He was immediately challenged by one of the maids. "Hey! You there. Aren't you one of his followers?" She flipped her thumb over her shoulder to where Jesus was being mocked and struck.

"Who, me? I just got here. I heard there was some kind of trial going on and I was curious. I don't know what you're talking about."

"Well, you sure look like a Galilean to me." The girl would not let it go.

"And you sound like one, too," another volunteered.

"I tell you, I'm not with him. So what if I'm a Galilean? I don't know that man at all." Peter flinched at the outright lie. Then he rationalized, *I thought I knew him, but apparently I didn't really.*

The heat warmed his body until the trembling almost stopped. Maybe everything would work out after all. Then another maid spoke, "You are one of them. I know I saw you with him."

Peter punched a fist into his other hand. "Woman, you are mad. You never saw me. Why, by the heavens and all the earth, I don't know what you're talking about. I do not know that man." He pointed to Jesus, who stood a few feet away, ropes around his wrists and thorns adorning his head. Peter's voice rose with each word so everyone turned to see what caused the commotion. Jesus also turned. Their eyes locked. In the distance Peter heard the crow of the rooster, calling the morning into being.

Horrified, Peter remembered Jesus' words predicting his denial. It was true. The prediction of his coming death must also be true. Tears spilled over his eyes and streamed down his face. He could do nothing but run – again.

Chapter One

Too Late

Encouraged by the confident call of the rooster, the sun rose boldly. Soft breezes swept away the chill of the night. Morning chores proceeded on schedule. Peter stood at a distance until close to noon when he had determined the fate of Jesus. Then, once again, his feet took him on a race to retreat from those sad, compassionate eyes.

He saw only blurred images as he ran down the cobblestone streets. Many shops were already closed for the noon meal and afternoon rest, while others were just pulling tent doors over their wares. A few defiantly stayed open, hoping for a few more customers from the city's many visitors.

Throughout Jerusalem Jews prepared for the Sabbath, while visitors were more anxious to see the current attraction – a crucifixion on Golgotha. Most people never witnessed a Roman crucifixion. Those who had seen one hoped for a more spectacular event – something to satisfy the craving for violence which must remain hidden in their own hearts.

In Peter's confused mind, it all seemed so unbearable. On the one hand there was Jesus, whose only crime was to love all people with an impossible love, and yet he was condemned to die. On the other hand, life sped on – work, play, rest, worship – as if nothing unusual was taking place.

Worship! How can those pious, religious leaders worship with a clear conscience? Peter's thoughts kept time with his racing feet. *How could they condemn a good man to death and then release an evil, rebellious leader of bandits and still worship as if all were well?*

Where is God? How can I ever pray again? And yet Peter found himself, over and over silently crying out, *Oh God! Oh God, help me!*

Heedless of people or animals, Peter took a corner so fast he barely missed the sharp edge of a building. His feet and thoughts raced on. A few heads turned as he passed, but most people seemed not to notice or care that a grown man was running like a lunatic through the streets of Jerusalem. Some looked for a pursuer, hoping for a battle. Seeing no one, they shrugged and returned to the task at hand.

Peter stumbled, caught himself against a building, and paused to catch his breath and gather his thoughts. A fisherman by trade until he left his nets to follow Jesus, Peter was used to physical activity. His normally tan, muscular body was paled and weakened by the former night's horrors. His dark, flashing eyes were dimmed and reddened as the unbidden tears of remorse continued to flow. He would rather find a cave and hide himself, but he was driven by some unfamiliar inner force to keep moving. Was it fear? Grief? Shame? He didn't know. His mind was not analytical like some of the others. He was too impulsive. And now the unfamiliar pulsating rhythm of his heart beat was forcing him to continue the race to that dread place of crucifixion, Golgotha.

He gathered all his available willpower and pushed himself away from the comfort of the cold, stone wall. In the distance sounds of the shouting crowds reached his pounding, straining ears. His feet rose and fell in rhythm with his racing heart, his sandals making soft, clapping sounds on the cobblestone, punctuating remembered words, "Crucify! Don't know him!"

Golgotha was his destination, whether by desire or by chance. *It really does look like a skull*, he thought. *Criminals are crucified there! But Jesus is not a criminal.* Words echoed fiercely in the cavernous recesses of his mind. Breath came in short gasps, but he didn't seem to notice. All that mattered was his destination. *I must get to Golgotha before they kill Jesus. Somehow, I must let him know how sorry I am.* Peter's thoughts kept his feet moving even though his muscles screamed for relief and rest.

Spurred by the increasing clamor ahead of him, Peter pushed on. Angry words pulsated in waves and attacked his straining ears – "Crucify" – "Son of God" – "healed" – "lame."

Lost in a labyrinth of thought, he nearly ran into a man and his donkey. The man shook his fist and hurled obscenities after the fleeing Peter, but nothing connected. Words were mere sounds mingling with an already jumbled commotion around him. It could just as well have been the donkey yelling at him.

A woman stepped from a door and Peter swerved to miss her. She turned and peered after him as if he were a mad man. Peter, himself, questioned his sanity, but continued to run. He would not – could not – stop.

"Watch where you're going, you big ox," the woman shouted. She then turned to her neighbors, who had gathered because of all the commotion, and babbled to them about a grown man running through the streets ignoring poor old women. Her words were lost in the wind as distance separated Peter from them.

A stray mongrel chased him, barking and snapping at his heels, but Peter seemed not to notice it. He was obsessed. He had to get to the place of the crucifixion before it was too late. Sounds of the angry mob drew him on like a magnet, pulling him closer and closer to the place he sought and yet did not want to find.

Catching his sandal on a loose stone in the path, Peter once again stumbled, lurched forward, righted himself before falling headlong on the road. His feet flying over the stones sent little cyclones of dust into the air in his wake. His breath was coming in such short, sharp gasps that he had to once again stop and wait for his lungs to fill with air. However, he dared wait only a few seconds. He must get to Golgotha in time. Still gasping for air, he pressed on.

Eyeing a long, narrow path snaking its way up the hill before him, Peter sighed and started up it. He half pulled and half dragged himself as he climbed the narrow path. It was a back way to the place of execution used by those who didn't want to be seen. The path was strewn with large stones and the low-hanging branches, making the ascent more difficult. Ignoring blood trickling down pricked fingers and scraped knees, Peter forced his trembling, weak legs to carry him forward. He could hear the loud, jeering crowd more clearly.

"He saved others. He cannot save himself."

"If he is the Son of God, let him come down."

"He said he would rebuild the temple in three days. Let him try it from the grave!"

At last, on the crest of the hill, he stared through the thickness of undergrowth at the sight before him. Three crosses standing upright, each lifting a man heavenward! He was too late! All the running, the racing, denying his lungs precious air they so desperately called for, and he was too late! Stark and cold against the noon-day sky, arms extended, three crosses sent shadows across the crowd of spectators. The earlier breeze died, leaving air stuffy, bereft of its life-giving oxygen.

Wearily Peter leaned against a gnarled olive tree as he waited for Jesus to die. Discouraged and numb, his mind wandered as he watched. He would rather not think at all, but how do you turn off your mind when it is so full of strange and awful events? Jesus was already on the cross. What more could he do? Reality of the truth struck him as forcefully as his earlier denial. He could do nothing. The salty taste of tears reached the corners of his mouth and continued down his beard.

Squeezing his eyes tightly closed, he let his body slowly slide to the ground. There he sat against the tree, trying unsuccessfully to turn off his racing thoughts. *Maybe if I can keep my eyes closed I won't have to see him. If I ignore those crosses, maybe I'll awake and find it's all a horrible dream.*

Peter, with all his rashness and quick actions, knew better. Even his eyes refused to obey his command to stay shut. He was compelled to look, and in so doing, felt himself pulled into those dark, sad eyes so full of pain. Even with Jesus on that cross, and him hiding in the undergrowth, Peter felt they were standing face to face. Was it his imagination, or was it simply a remembrance of the night before when he gazed into those eyes and heard the cock give its signal of a new day? Peter didn't know. Did it matter? The look he saw from the cross penetrated his soul anew. And once again the usually self-reliant, confident fisherman hung his head and wept bitterly. Torn between wanting to leave and needing to stay, Peter leaned helplessly against the trunk of the olive tree, feeling its bark press into his back.

To avoid the pain of watching his Master die, Peter began observing others who gathered near the cross. He was surprised to see so many. Some he knew, others were strangers to him. Most tried to stay out of the range of the soldiers who guarded their prisoners.

Such a mockery, Peter thought. *Soldiers in full uniform, swords in their sheaths ready for service, while their prisoners are fastened securely to crosses of execution. Do they really think one of them will come down and try to escape?* The thoughts sent more lines of anguish across his already anxious face.

Filled with remorse, anger and frustration, Peter found it difficult even to survey his surroundings. Hidden in the underbrush, he thought he could see without being seen, so with nothing or no one in mind, Peter stared at folks through the branches. John and Mary, the mother of Jesus, stood as close to the cross as the guards would permit. John had his arm protectively around the woman who gave birth to the man on the middle cross.[1]

John is different from the rest of us, thought Peter – *somehow more compassionate. He's a fisherman, also, but he sees things the rest of us miss – the beauty, the poetry, the spiritual. He's always the first to understand the riddles and jokes Jesus enjoyed telling. I'm glad he's there. At least someone has courage enough to be near.* An odd combination of regret, gratitude and envy surged through his soul.

The stones and twigs pressing into him, the smells of olives on the tree, and the total silence of nature all converged on Peter's consciousness as he continued to think and survey. The small, frail woman beside John again brought tears, but he tightly squeezed the salty liquid from his eyes and chanced another glance at Mary.

How can she bear to watch her son executed like a common criminal? But then again, how can she not be here? What must she be thinking? What must she think of me? I was so close and I deserted him – and her. Why can't I stop these painful thoughts?

Even in his grief, Peter admired the strength of the woman who stood her ground against the guards, or anyone who would try to send her away. Once again Peter felt a sense of gratitude for John, who protected her as much as possible and gave her what comfort he could. Even from his hiding place, Peter could sense the comfort Mary received from John's presence, and once again felt shame. He should be there.

Unable to stand the anguish any longer, Peter turned his dark, teary eyes away from them to his protector-tree. Seeking comfort, he hugged it like a long-lost friend until some semblance of composure could return. Taking a deep breath and swiping his arm across his eyes, he returned his gaze to others near the cross.

Who is that short, richly dressed man standing behind John and Mary? He looks like a member of the Sanhedrin, but why would he be here? He seems genuinely touched by this crucifixion, but if he's so concerned, why doesn't he do something to stop all this foolish waste of life?

Someone called out, "Nicodemus! There you are." Even though he strained to hear, the rest of their words were lost after Nicodemus replied, "Joseph, it's good to see you." The two men turned and walked away, deep in conversation. Peter was confused. *The man called Joseph must be rich and is possibly from the Sanhedrin as well. Why are they here?*[2]

Anxious thoughts churned within him until his head throbbed. Peter glanced toward the path he had ascended. *Maybe I should just leave. I can't stand to watch, but neither can I stand not to watch. What shall I do?*

Indecision faded as he slowly turned back to face the spectators on the opposite side – the far right of the cross. He was committed to watching. Two men, one elderly and the other much younger, huddled together with an elderly woman between them. The older man looked at least eighty years old, but was probably younger. A small man, his back was bent from years of obviously hard work. His hair and beard, more white than gray, complimented the tunic of rough dark brown or gray cloth. The color was not clear to Peter from his position by the olive tree. Had the man not shifted slightly, Peter might have thought him to be a wooden statue carved by the elements of time from an aged olive tree. Had Peter been watching earlier, he would have seen the man move with a slow, shuffling step.

The younger man, whom Peter assumed to be the son, was a little taller, but otherwise a younger version of the old man. His clothes also were dark brown with a rope of leather around his waist – similar to what he had seen on various beggars. Why would a beggar be here watching the execution? Surely he would gain no coins from this crowd.

The woman, about as broad as she was high, was also dressed in rough-woven clothes of brown, with a dark blue shawl around her head and shoulders, held by her tightly-clenched fists. Wisps of gray hair sneaked out around the edges. Even from the distance, Peter could see her divided concern for the older man and the younger one beside him.

Who are they? Peter's brow knit in concentration. Names evaded the digging, groping fingers into memory. Even from his screen of branches and leaves, Peter detected a sporadic sparkle in the corner of the younger man's eyes. *Tears, maybe? But why? And who are they? They look so familiar, especially the one who looks like a beggar. Where have I seen them before and why are they here?* Peter shook his head to fling the thoughts free from his confused, aching mind.

Convinced he could not be seen, Peter gained a little more courage and surveyed other spectators on the hill. As long as he watched people, he could keep his eyes off that middle cross.

Another man stood close to the older couple that he could not identify. And beside him was an even younger man, not much more than a boy. The older of the two was taller and more muscular than the youth. He had the look of a fisherman about him and seemed uncomfortable in these surroundings. His long, flowing brown coat was tied at the waist with cord. Peter recognized it as the kind used in making fishing nets. Wind tossed the dark, gray-speckled hair on his uncovered head.

The smooth face and youthful appearance made Peter believe the younger one was only in his mid-teens. He, too, was dressed in a light brown tunic covered by the brown, burlap-type material held in at the waist by cord. He was nervously pounding a fist into the palm of the other hand.

Such a young man, thought Peter. *Why would a father* – he assumed them to be father and son – *bring a young person to see men crucified?* The word crucified brought a new rush of unbidden tears. Swiping the back of his hand across his eyes, Peter tried once again to focus on the other people, anything to rid his mind of his reason for being there.

A woman and a little girl stood behind the man and boy. They were below most of the spectators where they could not really see all that was happening. Peter assumed they were with the man and boy. The woman was plump, but not overly so. Her dress was homespun cloth which draped her body with many folds, held by a band of blue at the waist. The shawl of off-white with blue trim around the edge covered her head. He could not see the dark eyes, but thought they must be filled with fear and anxiety. She held tightly to the little girl, who seemed interested in everything. Black hair like her mother's hung around her shoulders.

Why are they here? Children don't belong at executions. The young man can't be much more than fourteen, or so. And yet he seems much older. The child looks like she is a handful for the mother. Why are they here? But then, why are any of us here? Why is Jesus here?

Nothing made sense to him as, yet again, a flood of tears ran freely down his face. Waiting until he could see again, he continued his scrutiny. At the edge of the crowd, almost directly opposite himself, was a woman who was obviously from Samaria.

Why would a Samaritan woman be here? His confused, aching

head pounded with questions. *What reason could she possibly have? Could she be from that village of Sychar? Maybe...No, surely she's not the woman Jesus talked to at the well that day. It must be someone else.* As he remembered that hot day in Samaria beside Jacob's Well, his mind was filled with more frustration.

Shaking his head vigorously, Peter tried to physically shake the unwanted thoughts from his mind. It was impossible to focus. Drawing in a long breath, he realized he was still breathing hard, even though he had been sitting for a while. At least his lungs were not screaming in rebellious pain, but the long, deep breaths felt good. He was tired of trying to think anymore, tired of trying to make sense of anything. And yet, his mind could not let it go. He had to think. He had to wonder.

How could I, Peter the Rock, have fallen apart like I did? I was always strong and feared nothing – well, almost nothing. I would have taken on a whole army single-handed if necessary to save someone I loved. Didn't I draw my sword on the High Priest's slave in the garden? But Jesus didn't want that. He even spoke sharply to me. I was so sure I would be willing to die and would never desert my Lord, and yet, here I am sitting under this gnarled little tree, afraid to face my friends – if I have any left. I wonder if the tears will ever stop.

Struggling to pull aside a branch close to the ground, Peter looked for others he might know. From his vantage point, he could see Lazarus with his sisters, Mary and Martha. Both women were clinging to Lazarus for comfort. An arm around each of them, Lazarus watched the middle cross. Peter could see his face, but could not read the expression. It was almost as if he had a secret and was dying to tell it. Of course, he had been dead himself and Jesus brought him back to life.

That is something else that doesn't make sense, thought Peter. *It wasn't that long ago that Jesus brought Lazarus back from four days in the grave. But, now he can't – or won't – even bring himself down off that cross! Why? I don't understand. I just don't understand.*

Beside Lazarus, Martha, the older of the sisters, looked confused.

Her less-than-usual neat appearance seemed foreign. Mary, on the other side, had never been as tidy about her appearance, but also looked haggard and weary.

Once again Peter brushed his hand across his face, trying to collect his thoughts and at the same time stop the memories. Feeling a chill wind across his face, he noticed the sky growing black. Low, growling thunder moved toward Golgotha. The three crosses, which earlier had been silhouetted against a blue sky, were suddenly lost in blackness. Peter had never seen even treacherous storms, which arose suddenly on the Sea of Galilee, so black.

Peter pondered the approaching storm, wondering if he should leave. The decision was taken from him as the earth beneath him began to tremble. He could not leave. He rolled over to his knees and wrapped his arms around his tree for comfort. He would have called out, "Lord, save me," as he had done once long ago when Jesus had saved him from the raging sea, but it would have been a futile call. His Lord was on the cross and could not save him.

Peter tried to turn his head so that he could see what was happening at the cross, but all was lost in the blackness. Dark clouds began to send big, soaking drops of rain to the earth. In a matter of minutes, not a thread caught in the wet tears of nature remained dry. Darkness prevailed as the ground shook. The crowd, who had earlier cried for the life of Jesus, now cried out for help. Common sense would have driven the masses away, but fear held them glued to the earth. Like a wild animal tossing its prey, the earth tried to shake itself free of the mortal Sin.

Peter was sure the hill of Golgotha would split down the middle, swallowing them all in the cavernous bowls of the earth. Nothing could withstand that kind of violent shaking for long. Later he learned the veil of the temple did split in two. But at that moment, even though he wanted to run, all he could do was hold on to his tree and hope its roots would not give up their grip within the earth.

As suddenly as it began, the tremors stopped. Empty clouds hung low in the sky, and blackness, as dark as the death angel itself, persisted. For three hours the sun was held at bay and could not break through. So thick was the darkness one could almost feel its pressure. Only the soft murmurs which drifted like a rudderless ship gave any indication life still existed. No one had seen anything like this before. How could they know what to do? Would it last?

Most wanted to run to the safety of four solid walls they called home, to the light of their lamp, anything to dispel the utter and complete darkness, but no one could move. They could not even see their hands held up before fearful faces. A guard called for a torch, but who would, or could, find one to bring? The darkest night in anyone's memory had never been this black, or menacing, or chilling.

Peter held tightly to the olive tree as if his life depended on that attachment. The tree, silent and still, stood waiting with all the rest of creation. From the two side crosses came sobs of fear. From the center cross – not a sound. It was as if it did not exist. But Peter knew it did. It was there in the midst of the darkness of death.

Slowly the veil of black began to lift. The sun again began to shine, although somewhat paled. Peter reluctantly turned to gaze upon the center cross. Tears once again blurred his vision. He was indeed too late. It was finished.

Chapter Two

What Now?

Slowly the darkness dissipated like a morning mist of fog. With the light a perceived heat returned life to fear-frozen spectators. Glancing frantically here and there, they sought something familiar. Hands twitched, reaching out, testing their movement. Still too afraid to move, the spectators and guards alike stood rooted to the ground waiting for someone – anyone – to make the first move. Finally someone, or maybe several persons, gathered courage to test feet, lifting one, then the other. They were not rooted to the ground after all. Moving quickly, one foot then the other, they moved away from that dreadful place. Quickly the Place of the Skull lost its cloak of spectators, leaving it nearly naked in the aftermath of the storm. Only the guards and a few friends remained to cover its shame.

Stiff, aching fingers loosened their grip on the tree, and Peter again tried to sit with his back to the trunk. Twisting his body a little more, he could see the crosses. Three bodies were slumped forward, barely alive. Involuntarily he looked to the middle cross. Almost in a whisper, Jesus spoke, and while Peter could not hear, he knew it was finished.[1] Jesus shuddered, slumped forward, and died. Peter pulled at his already wild hair and wept yet another time.

How long Peter sat there, rocking his body back and forth and weeping, he did not know. Sounds from the direction of the cross drew his attention. He looked up to see the guards remove the body of Jesus from the grip of the nails. Nicodemus and Joseph of Arimathea were there to receive it.[2] Together they took the body to a nearby cave which belonged to Joseph. As he had done earlier, Peter followed at a distance to see where they were going.

He crept close and peered inside. Joseph and Nicodemus placed the body of Jesus on the stone bed. Peter watched as they hurriedly wrapped the body. It was nearing the hour of Sabbath. Fearing he would be caught as they came out of the cave, he crept softly away, glad that Joseph and Nicodemus had been responsible. It gave him some comfort to know that at least Jesus would not lie in a shallow grave in the Potter's Field.

Joseph and Nicodemus emerged from the cave, and several Roman soldiers rolled a huge stone over the entrance. There they stood guard. Peter heard them grumble, "Why are we going to so much trouble for a carpenter who got himself in trouble with the authorities?"

"Maybe they're afraid he'll walk away," laughed another. Hearty laughter from the rest followed.

"I still don't see why we have to sit here and guard the stupid stone," said another.

"The Jewish leaders are afraid the followers will come and steal the body."

"They and what army?" They laughed again. "No one's going to move that stone. Oh, well, we may as well get comfortable. It's going to be a long night."

The guards settled down with their gaming dice and were soon lost in their revelry and boisterous complaining about cheating and the cold. *If it weren't so tragic, it would be almost funny*, thought Peter. *We were all too afraid to even stand by him as he died; where would we get the courage to steal the body now that he's dead?*

With slow, shuffling steps, Peter began to retrace the path to Jerusalem. There was little strength left to pick his feet up and set them down again even in a slow walk. The sound of his scraping sandals echoed in the now nearly deserted streets.

For the first time in many days, Peter had to face his future. *Where will I go? What will I do? The last three years of my life were spent following Jesus because I thought he was the Messiah. Can I go back to Galilee and fish? Somehow that doesn't feel right.* He continued to move aimlessly toward Jerusalem.

"Peter! Simon Peter, wait up!" Peter turned, wondering if he really heard his name or if that too was an echo of the past. But there was John, with Mary still close by his side, coming down the street toward him, calling to him. He waited for them.

"Where are you going, Peter?" John asked as he approached the tear-streaked, bewildered man. Somehow neither of them looked like the confident disciples of a few days ago.

"I don't know," said Peter, too weary to even care that his face was still streaked with tears. His mind, too frustrated by questions and more questions, made his thoughts as fuzzy as his tear-dimmed vision.

"Come with us," said John, laying his hand on Peter's arm. Peter noticed that John, too, spoke with a husky voice and his face was also streaked with tears.

"Where are you going?" asked Peter.

"To my house in Jerusalem," said John. "Anyone is welcome. We'll observe the Sabbath, then spend the night of mourning together. When the new week begins, we'll go to the tomb and perhaps move his body to a more permanent place. Joseph has only loaned the tomb."

"I don't want to be a burden to anyone," said Peter weakly. The words sounded strange, even to his own ears. John looked surprised, then, trying to choke back laughter, said, "Since when have you been concerned about such things? Come on. We're all friends. Let's wait together."

"Yes, come with us, Simon Peter," said Mary. She laid a hand on his arm. "We need to be together."

John tugged at Peter's sleeve and started off to his house. Peter fell into step beside them. The once busy streets were almost empty. Only zombie-like spectators from Golgotha silently hurried to find some safe place to go. Some had been there out of curiosity, some because of grief. The mob's crying, "Crucify him!" no longer reverberated through the streets, but echoed in the minds. As if anxious to put the horror of the day to rest, the sun slid toward the horizon. John, Peter and Mary made their way toward the house that

John called home when he was in Jerusalem. It had belonged to a distant cousin, who, having no other family, gave it to John before he died a year or so earlier. It was not far from Golgotha, and they arrived in time to observe the rituals of the Sabbath. However, without Jesus to bless the bread, it just wasn't the same. That night and the next day passed quietly. By the following evening, more friends found their way to John's house, where they would wait together for the dawn.

Mary and Martha arrived with their brother Lazarus. "We brought spices for the burial," said Mary as John greeted them at the door.

"Thank you, Mary. We'll have to wait for morning. I'm sure the guards won't allow us to go into the tomb tonight."

"What will we do until morning?" asked Martha. She had learned to slow down a little, but under pressure she preferred to be busy doing something.

Lazarus smiled at her the way he used to do when he teased her as a child. "Maybe you and Mary can whip up a snack. Jesus' mother shouldn't have to provide for guests in John's home, and I have a feeling we'll have a house full before long."

"Really?" asked Martha. "Who else is coming?"

Before Lazarus could answer, John was opening the door for more folks. Peter, still smarting from his own feelings of guilt and shame, watched from a dimly lit corner as the little house began to seem crowded to him. It was not really a tiny house in comparison to some, but it was not a large house either. He would have preferred to have only the disciples and family members present on this last night of mourning before their final farewell, but it was not his decision. He began to project his internal anger at himself onto others, keeping it in check only because he was a guest in John's home.

"Are you sure it's all right for me to be here?" Peter turned to see who the woman was, since the voice was not familiar. *It's that woman from Samaria! What's she doing here? Surely John will not let her stay.* Peter stared, disbelief in his very stance. But even as the thoughts rumbled around in his frustrated and perplexed mind, John stepped aside for her. Seeing the displeasure in Peter's eyes, the woman almost turned to leave.

"Don't let him bother you," said Andrew, Peter's brother. He took her by the arm and led her to the other women. "His scowl is much worse than his actions. You loved Jesus. That's all that counts tonight."

"Thank you, Andrew," she said, as she moved to greet Mary, Jesus' mother, then offered to help Martha and her sister, Mary. They had begun to prepare many items brought by the mourners. There were the usual liquids – wine, milk and water – as well as cheese, meat, fruit, and bread. No one was really hungry since they had just eaten the Sabbath meal, but nervous energy created the need to at least have something on which to nibble, or a cup from which to sip.

Peter watched the women performing their tasks as if nothing unusual was happening. His attention was drawn back to the door as John admitted the elderly couple and younger man whom Peter had seen at Golgotha. The younger man's eyes did sparkle. Peter wasn't sure who he was and really didn't want to know. *Why is John allowing all these outsiders to intrude on our grief?* Shaking his head in confusion, Peter turned away and stared out the window while John welcomed them into his home.

Next the family with the little girl entered. *Now this is really too much! Surely John knows a child doesn't belong here. We'll probably be up all night!* But they found a bench, and the men and little girl sat down while the woman moved to help, offering some meal and oil she had brought.

Peter paced slowly in a corner of the room, taking only one or two small steps, turning and retracing them. He combed his fingers through his hair in rhythm with his feet as he walked, hoping he could pull some of the tangled thoughts from his tortured mind. *Maybe I should leave*, he thought. *I don't belong here with all these people. I need to be alone with my grief.* His feet would not follow his head's suggestion.

And then came the final blow! John opened the door to the two richly-robed members of the Sanhedrin. *How can he do that? They're the very ones who killed Jesus!* Peter's anger was at the boiling point.

He was on the verge of saying something when the child in the opposite corner distracted him.

"Who are the men in the pretty robes?" she asked innocently.

Don't parents teach their children to be seen and not heard? Peter turned back to express his anger, but by then the men had moved to a bench, and the anger had lost its momentum.

Like the miracle of the feeding of the five thousand from two loaves and five fishes, the house seemed to stretch and bulge as more folks arrived, still leaving room to move around. They mingled somewhat, talking in soft, hushed tones, afraid of the sound of their own voices. When the dawn came, they would scatter like chaff in the wind.

Some wanted only a place to sit in silence where they could remember. A corner spot provided enough solitude for one or two who sought to erase the numbness, thoughts pulled inward. Remembrance was important, and yet to forget would have seemed less painful. Peter chose to walk away his grief, taking a few steps in one direction and then retracing them to the point of beginning.

One or two others went to the courtyard in back, which was surrounded by a stone wall enclosing a few small trees and some flowers. Above the soft squeaking of leather sandals and the slap of footsteps, a hum of whispered voices rose and fell in an eerie sort of rhythm.

While Martha and the other women were preparing refreshments, a comfortable chair was placed beside a window for Mary, Jesus' mother. A slight breeze blew through the open space and even though she could see nothing in the dark, Mary knew the cobblestone walkway was there. She wanted a connection with the outside – if only as a memory. Everyone tried to make her as comfortable as possible. The rest of the women would keep busy so the night would not seem so long. Whatever task they chose to while away the time, each one was determined to linger, waiting for the sunrise to end her vigil.

Along the wall behind the chair where Mary sat, an assortment of benches, stools and chairs were haphazardly placed, giving the room a scattered look. At the back of the room were more chairs and benches, leaving only enough space in front of the narrow door for passage to and from the garden.

For a while the murmuring voices dropped to a mere whisper as grief was pulled inward. Only the almost imperceptible movement could be heard from the women who filled cups and offered bits of fruit or cheese.

Twilight faded into darkness as the sun drifted silently, noiselessly over the horizon. Lamps were soon lit and candles placed around the room. The long wait for dawn began in earnest. The sharp edge of grief became tempered by time and the comfort of friends gathered in mutual sadness. Voices rose and fell in an odd sort of rhythm, as once again questions with no answers were asked and comments which expected no response were expressed.

Chapter Three

Early Memories

Simon Peter struggled with unfamiliar feelings which were becoming all too familiar. He was in a situation not very much to his liking. *Should I stay where I feel uncomfortable, or should I leave and be alone, and probably be even more uncomfortable? I've always felt quite at home here. I'm glad John asked me to come. I just wish I could rid myself of that nagging guilt.* Peter made his choice to stay even without being fully aware of having done so. He limited his pacing to a step or two, but it helped him to forget others were present. His steps and thoughts kept a rhythm of their own making.

Peter, startled by a hand on his shoulder, turned abruptly, fist raised to defend himself. John ducked as Peter swung around. "Hold on there, Peter. I'm your friend, remember?"

Embarrassed, Peter glanced quickly to see if anyone else had seen his fearful reaction. If anyone did, it was ignored.

"Sorry John. I was lost in thought and...well, I'm sorry."

"Do you need anything, Peter? You know, we're all struggling with the events of the last few days, but you look like a volcano about to erupt."

"No, I'm fine. I was just wondering...that is..." Peter, never at a loss for words, found it difficult to put his thoughts into words. "I was loyal and true – at least most of the time, wasn't I?" He didn't wait for a response. Once the flow began, words tumbled freely out of his mouth. "I thought I was one of Jesus' closest friends, and yet I wonder now if I ever really knew him. It seemed I was always misunderstanding him, especially when it was crucial that I should comprehend the meaning his words. Will I ever understand him, John? Or does it even matter now that he's dead?"

"Peter, none of us really knew him, or were sure of his teachings. We tried, but...well...he was just so different."

"But you always seemed to catch on more quickly than the rest of us." It wasn't an angry or jealous accusation, but simply a statement of truth.

"Not really, Peter." John felt self-conscious. He knew he could grasp the meaning of riddles and parables when the others couldn't, but that didn't make him better. "We're just different, you and I, Peter. You're far more willing to go out on a limb than I am."

"You mean I'm quick to act and I speak without thinking. Yeah, I know, but still...I guess I need to think now, and that's not easy for me. I feel agitated. I need to move a little. Even though I can only take a few steps, it somehow helps me think." Peter looked helplessly to John. He wondered if he sounded like a fool.

John again laid his hand on Peter's shoulder. "I understand, Peter. It's been hard for all of us. Changes are coming too fast. We need to pool our memories." He gave Peter a friendly pat on the back and moved on to talk to someone else. Peter returned to this thoughts, moving slowly back and forth. He paused and glanced from one to another. *We're a strange mix*, he thought. *Jesus touched so many people.* Fresh tears filled his eyes as he looked toward Mary in her gray-blue dress with the worn, pale ivory-colored shawl wrapped tightly around her shoulders. Her gray hair, still long and beautiful, framed her face, which seemed peaceful even in her agony of grief. She appeared unaware of all the chatter and hum of conversation, but feeling Peter's eyes upon her, turned to face him. Their eyes met and she smiled a faint, fragile smile. Peter could not stand that look of compassion that was so much like her son's. He turned away, swiping at his eyes with his sleeve.

John once again appeared at his side, offering him a cup of something hot. He took it but did not drink right away. "Thanks, John." Nodding to the family near Mary, he asked, "Who is that man, and why does he have children here?" His attempt to keep the irritable edge from his voice was not very successful.

"His name is Saul from Galilee. He's a fisherman," John replied.

Saul, sensing Peter's gaze, unconsciously pulled at the cord holding his brown coat in place at his waist. Suddenly aware of his behavior, he stopped, running brown, large-knuckled hands through dark, gray-speckled hair. He would have given a boatload of fish to be out on his beloved sea at that moment.

John continued, "The young boy next to him is his son, Adam." Adam was a handsome youth, reflecting his father's image as he must have looked at a much younger age. Dark, unruly hair often fell over his dark flashing eyes, which followed Peter's gaze. He was developing the muscles of a fisherman – muscles which, this night, were tense as he clenched and unclenched his fists, trying to be an adult in a youth's body. He had removed his outer brown coat. In the semi-darkness of the room, his complexion looked even darker than the tanned skin which he had gotten fishing with his father.

"Adam has been changed by the few encounters he had with Jesus. He may look like a boy, but believe me, Peter, he's suffering like the rest of us," John continued. "On the other side of Adam is his mother. Miriam has been Saul's wife since she was fourteen. I've never heard her complain, and she keeps a motherly eye on her husband and her children. She met Jesus and knows that Adam will follow his teachings. That does not displease nor disappoint her. Adam is a good boy. He will do the right thing. Saul hoped they would become a father-son team. But now...well, she's here to support them both. Beside her is their daughter, Leah, who is about six and a half years old, going on fifteen sometimes."

Leah looked more like her mother than her father, a little chubby but not overly heavy. She had the face of a cherub outlined by long, dark hair. Big, round, dark eyes, which at times seemed black, were emphasized by long, curling eyelashes. The little pug nose wrinkled like a rabbit when she was curious about something, which was often. She stayed close to her mother while she tightly clutched a straw doll that Adam made for her.

John smiled at Peter. "I know you don't care a great deal for kids, but these are unusual times. All memories are important for us – even ones from the children."

"Mommy, why is that man staring at us?" the child asked.

Embarrassed, her mother drew her closer. "Shhh. That's Simon Peter, one of Jesus' disciples. I don't think he believes children should be here."

"Well, I don't care what he thinks," answered the little girl defiantly. "Jesus was my friend, too!" Then she added softly, almost pleadingly, "Wasn't he?"

"Of course he was your friend, too. Now, close your eyes and sleep awhile," Miriam said quietly as she pulled the child closer to her.

Peter could not help but hear the conversation. He scowled at them, but John chuckled to himself and moved away. Peter watched the women move quietly around the room, filling cups, offering bread, cheese and fruit. He almost envied them – although he would never admit it, even to himself. At least they had something to do. When the hands were busy, it seemed the mind lingered less on grief. In truth, Mary, who cared little for chores of the kitchen, lent a helping hand to her sister, Martha, just for that very reason – to keep too busy to think!

Mary took something to her brother, Lazarus; Peter couldn't see what. Again he felt the sharp pang of grief as he watched the two of them teasing each other like children. *Lazarus should be dead,* he thought, *but here he is. He's been our friend for a long time. We used to tease him because he didn't like fishing.* Peter smiled to himself at the memory of them ribbing Lazarus. *He was always reading or studying something. I expect he would have become a priest if he could have brought his beliefs into harmony with those of the religious leaders.*

Peter turned his back on the friends from Bethany as he paced his two or three steps. *I just don't understand. Why is Lazarus alive and Jesus lying out there in that cold tomb? Not that I want Lazarus to be dead, but...Oh, I just don't know what I mean, except Jesus was to lead us and now he is gone.*

Peter's footsteps fell heavily as if kicking stones. He realized the others had stopped talking and were watching him. He stopped, shrugged, and made some kind of unintelligible comment that could have been, "Sorry." Slowing his measured steps, he hoped to pull his thoughts to a quieter tone.

He continued to survey the room full of people. Curiosity had pulled some of the mourners from their normal reserve. They were a strange group – men, women, rich, poor, old, young. He noticed some tried to look without staring at Nicodemus, Joseph of Arimathea, and the Samaritan woman, probably the three most unexpected guests present. The two men were obviously dressed in a much richer fashion than the rest of them, and the woman was conspicuously a Samaritan.

"Why are they here?" Peter asked his brother, who approached and stood beside him. Andrew turned his gaze in the direction of Peter's glare.

"Who do you mean? There's a room full of people here." Andrew knew who he meant, but liked to tease his brother

Irritated with Andrew, Peter's voice was a little sharp. "You know who I mean – them!" He nodded toward Nicodemus and Joseph. "They stick out like sore thumbs in all their finery!"

"Why, Peter," Andrew said with as straight a face as he could muster, but unable to hide the twinkle in his eye, "that sounded a little like prejudice. Joseph provided a place for Jesus when they took him off the cross."

"Well, they don't belong here," Peter growled and glared at Andrew, who turned and walked away, smiling to himself. Peter clenched his teeth and tried to think. He opened his mouth to speak, but closed it without a word. After several such start-stop attempts, he finally began to speak softly – more to himself than to anyone in particular.

"Jesus and I really were good friends. Even before he left Nazareth, we knew each other. Sometimes he went fishing with us when his work was caught up at the carpenter's shop."

He stopped talking and paced a couple of steps. No one commented. They listened and waited for him to continue his story

– or not. It was a night for waiting. No one was in a hurry.

Peter stopped walking and looked around the room, searching for even he knew not what. "Once he even tried to teach me carpentry." There was another long pause before he continued. A smothered snickering sound came from somewhere near the table where his brother, Andrew, stood filling his cup. He turned to face Peter, quickly placing a hand over the grin. He remembered the story. Nodding to his brother, he returned to his seat.

Peter pulled at the corners of his mouth as a small smile tried to escape. He didn't want to smile. This was a time of grief and somberness. Memory, however, would not let him immerse completely in gloom, and he smiled in spite of himself.

Sighing deeply, he continued. "I banged my thumb instead of a nail," he said. "I was so angry that I started to throw the hammer." Peter turned toward the window to hide his smile. With his back to the room, he continued. "Jesus stopped me. He told me not to blame the hammer for my mistake. Then he..." Peter paused again, trying to untangle the words which formed a lump in his throat. Pushing aside the lump, he continued hoarsely. "He healed my throbbing thumb and laughed, telling me to stay with fishing. He hesitated and then added, 'for awhile.' The healing surprised me, but I thought I must have been mistaken about the pain. Maybe it didn't hurt as much as I thought it did."

James and John sat together in a corner of the room talking quietly to each other. When Peter began to talk, they stopped to listen. The three of them had been so close to each other and to Jesus. Floods of memories rushed in.

"Remember how we were a threesome?" Peter asked, turning to face the Zebedee brothers. "We were with Jesus almost everywhere he went. Just a couple of nights ago we were in the garden with him."

James and John nodded. "Yes, it was only a couple of nights ago. We didn't do so well with our own prayers." James looked a little embarrassed.

"No," added John, "but Jesus understood."

Peter stared at the cup in his hand, turning it over and over. "You are both fishermen like me. But you're different, John – more reflective. You treasured those conversations which seemed to elude the rest of us. You seemed to be at home with the spiritual side of Jesus, while the rest of us struggled. Even so, did you really understand him?" In his grief Peter had forgotten their earlier conversation.

"No one fully understood Jesus," John reminded him. "He was so far ahead of us spiritually, how could we understand? Maybe if we had a few more years..." John shrugged his shoulders. There really was no point in finishing his sentence.

Around the room, the murmurs, which rose and fell as the mourners shared stories with one another, slowly died away when they heard Peter speaking. While he didn't speak to the entire group, all listened.

"Do you remember when we all walked down to the river to see John the Baptizer?" asked Peter, another small smile playing around the corners of his mouth.[1]

"Remember?" answered James. "How could we forget? The loud, booming voice of that wild-looking man echoed across the valley like thunder on a summer night."

"His message was clear, short and to the point," said his brother. "Remember how he shouted, 'The time is drawing near. Repent! Be baptized for your sins.'" John raised his voice so much that some glanced at the door in alarm. Would the sound bring the Roman soldiers running? Fear sent a trickle of sweat down foreheads and backs. Thomas moved quickly and quietly to the door, opened it a crack, and listened. Hearing nothing unusual, he softly closed the door and leaned with his back against it.

"Sorry," said John, lowering his voice and glancing toward Thomas. "I guess I got a little carried away."

"Why is everyone so afraid?" asked the little girl, lifting her head from her mother's lap.

Embarrassed that her child had spoken, Miriam whispered loudly, "Shush! We will talk later."

"But I want..."

"Shush! Later."

James and John had turned with the rest to see the child, who was so bold and unafraid. They couldn't help smiling.

"She's right," said James. "Why are we afraid? Surely the soldiers won't come into a home in the middle of the night and arrest us simply because we knew him!"

"I wouldn't be too sure of that," said Thomas. "They didn't hesitate to take Jesus unarmed from the garden in the middle of the night."

While some webs of doubt had been brushed aside, other threads were left dangling, teasing the memories. The cadence of whispered sounds rose and fell in rhythm once again as each became lost in thought.

Chapter Four

Memories of Temptation

Without intending to do so, Peter opened the floodgate of memory and gave permission for others to share memories. Like the smell of pungent food cooking to a hungry person, the mention of John the Baptist reminded them of their hunger to hear and tell stories and experiences of Jesus. Without realizing it, the first step was taken away from the deep grief toward a hope-filled tomorrow.

Many memories of John the Baptist surfaced. Those who heard him could picture it clearly. Those who hadn't heard him could only speculate about how it must have been. Closing his eyes, Peter could almost hear the water lapping at the shore of the Jordan River. James, whose thoughts paralleled Peter's, spoke quietly, "I can almost hear the call of the birds and feel the cool breeze blowing across the river."

"What I remember most clearly," John spoke more softly now, "was Jesus stepping down into the river facing John. I can still see the hesitancy on John's face, almost as if he felt he was not worthy to baptize Jesus."

James said, "Can you really blame him? None of us understood why Jesus even went to the river. Surely he, of all people, needed no repentance or baptism."

"That's true," said John. "Remember the deep, thunderous voice out of the sky? It said, 'This is my Son. I am pleased with him.' [1] A shimmering dove-like image hovered over Jesus. Later, he told us the time was drawing near," said John. "Even though many of you call me a *thinker*, I had no idea what he meant."

Peter stood staring down at James and John – from one to the other and back again. Finally, fixing his gaze on the older brother, he asked, "What do you think now, John? We all thought Jesus was the long-awaited Messiah. Even when he was here, and we followed him, sometimes it didn't seem possible, but..." Peter's voice trailed off, leaving the question unasked.

"You're right, Peter," spoke John in his rich, deep voice, raising his head so their eyes met. "We thought after working in Joseph's carpenter shop so long Jesus would be anxious to get on with building his kingdom." He lowered his gaze, slowly shaking his head to clear his thoughts. "His baptism was confusing and made little sense to most of us, but it did seem like a good turning point – a beginning. I thought maybe it meant the time was right – you know, time to begin his Kingdom. But when he turned toward the desert wilderness instead of Jerusalem, I was even more confused."

Once again John shook his head slowly, bringing his focus back to the present. "It didn't make sense to any of us." He paused, stood for a minute, then moved to look out the window – not that he could see anything. He turned back to face eager, expectant faces. "Once, when Jesus and I were alone after his return from the desert, I asked him about his experiences in the wilderness. I wanted to know why he went away, what he did and how he survived." John stared blankly as if he could see into the past.

Blinking and bringing his thoughts back to the present, he continued, "Jesus reminded me he would leave almost thirty years of experiences with friends and family. Can you imagine how hard it would be to live in one place for thirty years and then give it all up? Even Jesus couldn't turn his back on family and friends without some pain, grief, and soul-searching."

Mary turned from her pondering of the darkness, a sad smile on her face. *He understands so much about my son*, she thought. *No wonder Jesus gave us to each other at his death*. John, seeing her turn, waited for her to speak, but words were not there. Only thoughts filled her consciousness. *Yes, it was hard, not only for Jesus, but for me and his brothers and sisters as well. I knew the moment he turned and walked with assurance toward the desert I had lost him.* Mary turned back to the window and continued to stare into the night. John returned to his story.

"Even though Jesus was the Son of God, he was in human flesh. He breathed, hurt, and felt the same emotions we all feel. That's why he was so understanding. He seemed to know my thoughts, even when I couldn't find words to express them.

"Do you remember how often he talked about a journey to Jerusalem?" They all nodded. "Well, he knew he would have to leave his family and friends, the security and love he knew. He always knew he would have to do that, but when the time came, it was still hard for him."

Some knew about the temptations in the wilderness.[2] They knew it was a rough time for Jesus, one he didn't talk about. Not only were they curious, but they longed for memories to keep him alive among them.

John turned, walked to the table, poured a cup of wine, and picked up a piece of cheese. He wasn't hungry, but needed to be doing something. "Jesus said he needed time alone to think and meditate. He had many decisions and plans to make. His struggles became so intense that he lost track of time. Forty days and nights were long enough to resolve his conflicts and answer many questions."

"What kind of questions?" asked Andrew. "I thought he always had it all together. He seemed never to be lost or flailing the way the rest of us did."

"That's because he settled the hard questions before his ministry," said John. "Questions like: How was he supposed to accomplish his task? Who would help him? Where would he begin? How long would it be? A lot of soul searching was necessary – even for Jesus. I don't think any of us ever realized how urgent and intense his struggles were. There was so much to accomplish in such a short time."

"It didn't have to be such a short time," said Thomas. "If only he had listened to us..."

Understanding his frustration, John nodded to Thomas as his words faded. He lifted his cup and took a long, gulping drink. The conversation with Jesus came back to him. "But he had to listen to

God first – not us."

Thomas was not satisfied with that answer, but he knew he would never be satisfied.

Quietly John moved closer to Mary and eased himself onto a chair near her. Glancing at her protectively he said, "It must have been really difficult for him. He not only had to search his own soul for the way God wanted him to proceed, but Satan was there at every turn to stop him. When you think about it, it's a little ironic. The quietest, most peaceful place in the world became the most important and intense battlefield of his life. Jesus wrestled with temptations Satan threw at him, one by one. None of us could have held up like he did. We would have given in very quickly."

Leah, wide awake, knew she should be quiet, but her inquisitive, active mind seemed to always race with questions. She could keep quiet no longer. She wanted to know things – anything! Even as her brother tried to keep her from speaking, she managed one question: "What are temptations?"

John glanced at the bold little girl. He thought she was probably too young to know she should keep quiet and yet old enough to be curious. He tried to hide a smile of amusement at the embarrassment of her family.

Peter was not as tolerant as John. He turned to the child. "Who *are* you? Don't you know children should be seen and not heard?" His voice had a sharp, abrasive edge to it which would have sent most children to their mama in tears. But Leah was not like most children.

"My name is Leah," she answered, staring into his eyes, daring him to contradict her. "I'm here with my brother and mother and father because Jesus was our friend. And I just want to know what everyone is talking about."

Before Peter could say anything more, John interrupted. "It's all right, Peter. She is young, but... well, we're living in strange times. For tonight, at least, we may as well forget age, gender and position in life. We're all grieving and looking for memories to give us comfort."

Peter glared, shrugged his shoulders, and returned to his pacing. *It's his house*, he thought. *If he wants to let children act like adults, that's his business. But I don't have to like it!* His feet lifted and fell a little more heavily as he measured his space, sandals slapping the floor like punctuation marks.

John understood Peter's feelings of anger and frustration. Life was changing too rapidly for all of them, but the child also had a need for answers and her parents for understanding. Trying to be sensitive to all of them, he decided to treat her question in the same manner he would each person there. Leah might be a child, but she deserved straightforward answers the same as the adults.

"Temptations were...are...ideas that seem good, but are really bad," he began. "Satan tried to get Jesus to accept evil as good. The Tempter, as Satan is sometimes called, first of all tried to convince Jesus that he wasn't the Son of God at all. Satan told him if he was really the Son of God he could turn the stones to bread. You see, Satan was hoping for some tiny shadow of doubt which might be hiding in Jesus' mind. '*If* you are the Son of God,' he said, and for a split second the human mind of Jesus thought, maybe I just thought I heard a voice at my baptism."

"But Jesus didn't really believe him, did he?" Leah's dark eyes were wide and questioning. She was completely absorbed in John's story and she couldn't bear to think Satan had tricked Jesus into believing him.

"Well," John continued, amazed at the innocence and curiosity with which the child wanted to know more, "Satan handed him a small stone and urged him to do it. He knew how hungry and weary Jesus was. The thought of food would sound pretty good. He reminded Jesus of his humanness, and his desire of a home, family, security, love, like anyone else. It would have been easy to go back to Nazareth, maybe eventually get married, preach a little at home, and work in his synagogue. Satan tried hard to convince Jesus it was God's will for his life." Pausing briefly, John wistfully glanced at Thomas. "If only he had gone back..."

"But he didn't, did he?" Leah commented with a sound of

smugness that sounded more like, "I knew it all the time!"

John smiled as he sighed deeply and glanced at Peter. He knew the *if only* could never be true. Peter also sighed and shook his head back and forth slowly as John picked up the threads of the story. "No, Jesus didn't do it, but he told me it helped him understand better how we humans are so often tempted to turn our own stones to bread and look for present comfort, forgetting the future needs."

Silence hung over the room as John paused. Leah slipped away from her mother and stood beside John, looking expectantly at him. Regaining his train of thought, John continued to speak softly, reflectively. "Then Jesus said Satan tried another temptation. Since Jesus didn't fall for the first one, Satan suggested he throw himself from the pinnacle of the temple in Jerusalem."

"What's a pinnacle?" asked Leah.

"It's the very highest point of something – in this case the temple in Jerusalem. It's also the highest point in the city." John watched Leah to see if she understood. She nodded, so he moved on. "Satan believed it was the desire of all humans – Jesus included – to obtain immortality – that means to live forever. He reasoned that if Jesus was really the Son of God, then he was already immortal and nothing would happen to him. But, if he was only human, he would jump at the chance for immortality."

John smiled at the little girl who still stood beside him. She was enjoying being in the adult world and didn't seem to notice her brother's embarrassment.

John placed an arm around the child as he continued his story. "Jesus really didn't want to experience pain or death any more than any of us do. He had a human body like ours. We all witnessed his human pain on Golgotha."

Even though Mary had not turned toward them, she had heard and pondered everything the way she had always done. "He certainly had his share of cuts and bruises as a boy growing up around a carpenter's shop." The softness of Mary's voice startled John and he turned toward her. She still faced the window, staring into the darkness, almost as if unaware of anyone's presence. However, they all knew she was aware.

"He was well acquainted with grief," she continued so softly John had to strain to hear her. "He saw people die – people he loved – grandparents, and even Joseph." John waited, giving her time to respond further. When she didn't, he returned to his remembrances.

Leah opened her mouth to speak, but her brother's glare made her think again. John, anticipating her question, smiled at her and said, "No, Leah, Jesus didn't jump. He didn't need to prove his relationship to God – not to Satan, not to himself, not to anyone. They both knew he was who he said he was."

"I knew it," she said smugly and leaned closer to John.

"No, the Tempter could not convince Jesus with either of those arguments," continued John, "so he tried a third time. This time he told Jesus he could become the master of all the kingdoms of the world. He would only have to worship Satan."

"Oh," whispered Leah. "He didn't, did he?" She was pretty sure, but doubt clouded her certainty.

"No," John reassured her. "He didn't. But imagine what it would be like to have that kind of power. Everyone expected the Messiah to be a powerful King, so who would ever know? However, Jesus didn't need power from Satan."

"He had God's Power, didn't he?" Leah stated as if she had experienced his power herself.

"That's right. He had a far greater power," John replied.

Andrew, listening intently, was fascinated by John's story, aided by the child that no one seemed to know, other than her name. "So, why didn't he use the power he had? Why did he allow the Roman soldiers to arrest him? Why did he allow them to...?" He couldn't bring himself to finish his question. Everyone knew what he wanted to say. They also wondered why Jesus didn't use his power to save himself.

Peter stood unmoving, his attention fixed on John and Andrew. He also wondered why.

"Because he loved us." The statement was so soft John wasn't sure it had come from the little girl. *A little child shall lead us*, he thought as he took another sip of his drink.[3]

"That's right, Leah." He smiled at her. "They were all serious temptations. None of us could have been as strong as he was, and I told him so. But he loved us enough to go through them for us."

John paused, considering what to say next, then he continued, "Jesus said the problem with temptations is that there is always a small grain of truth in them, which leads us to believe we are doing the right thing – even if it is wrong."

Adam, gaining confidence by his sister's acceptance, moved a little closer to John. "But how did Jesus handle all of those temptations? I know he refused them, but how? It seems he was being asked to back away from the very will of God. Surely he was the Son of God. Couldn't he have just called on the angels to protect him? Or maybe he could have, you know, snapped his fingers and the Tempter and the temptations would be gone."

Peter turned and looked at the youth in surprise. His surprise turned to amazement. *What is going on here? What's with the youth of today? First the little girl, and now this young man! How does one so young dare to speak as an equal with the adults in the room? And where do they get such maturity of thought and knowledge?* Peter couldn't admit even to himself the twinge of envy he felt for the knowledge and courage of the boy. He glared at the youth who would not back down. He opened his mouth, intending to tell the boy to sit down. John, sensing his thoughts, smiled and motioned for Peter to hold his tongue.

"You're Leah's brother." It was not a question, but simply an acknowledgment.

"That's right," said the suddenly shy youth. "I'm Adam. And..." He paused and then went on rapidly and breathlessly, "I'm sorry if we're outspoken. But I guess my sister is right *this* time." He glanced down at his sister, who smiled adoringly at him. "We just want to know more about our friend."

John answered the boy, "That's really why we're all here." He paused briefly. "It's true Jesus was the Son of God, but he was also human. He wanted to leave us some guidelines to follow. It was the human side of Jesus that Satan attacked. He knew he could not touch the Spiritual realm. These were all human, physical temptations – the same kind we all face. And Jesus fought them with human, physical means – the Word of God, the Scriptures, the Torah."

"The Torah?" asked Adam, surprised at such a simple solution.

"Yes," answered John. "The Torah. Its teachings are available to all of us. You see, the first temptation was to turn the stones to bread. Jesus answered from our Scriptures. He said that people cannot live on just bread.[4] The second was to throw himself from the pinnacle. He answered once more from the Scriptures. He reminded Satan that the Scriptures say we should not tempt the Lord our God.[5] The third was to receive all the kingdoms of the world. And the third time Jesus told him to go away because our Scripture says we should worship the Lord our God, who is the only one we will serve."[6]

The young man was amazed. "Jesus really knew his Torah in order to remember the words when he was so hungry and cold and lonely."

John smiled and winked at Lazarus who had gotten up to stretch his legs. "They were very much a part of his life. Even in the worst time of struggle and temptation, they came easily to his memory. He knew what God said through the prophets. And you're right. Jesus learned them by choosing to study God's word. Then he reflected on that word in communication with God, his Father. It was his way of overcoming temptation. He left that as a guide for us in our time of temptation."

"That's right," said Mary, who turned away from her steady gaze into the darkness and faced them. "Whenever I wanted him for something, he could usually be found in the Synagogue studying, or on the mountain studying, or in the corner of the carpenter shop studying." She laughed softly at the memory. "He was always studying. Maybe Lazarus will tell you how much he loved the temple."

Adam nodded and glanced at Lazarus, who said, "Maybe later." Adam was content for the present. He turned to the table and picked up some cheese and bread. Then he took his sister's hand.

"I think you've been a pest long enough," he said.

"But I ..." Leah started to protest. Adam gave her some bread and cheese and nudged her toward her father. He would wait for Lazarus' story, which he sensed would be told before the night was over.

For a time each was lost in memories not ready to be shared. As the night moved toward the midnight hour, sounds from the Jerusalem streets had softened to only a few stray dogs barking and other normal night sounds.

Chapter Five

Get Behind Me

Outside the house, stars twinkled and the moon tried valiantly to shed some light in a darkened world. Inside, flickering candles and oil lamps did their best to drive away the darkness that threatened the mourning souls. Peter paced in his self-appointed two-foot square of space. Of all the grieving friends, he was sure he had the most for which to be sorry. They all fled in fear, but he denied even knowing Jesus when he was cornered. At least John's courage returned enough to support Mary in her darkest hour. Talking was difficult for Peter, but thinking was even more troublesome. He struggled with emotions he never knew he had. He understood Jesus in death even less than in life.

Mulling John's words over in his mind, Peter spoke – more to himself than to anyone in particular. "That was a difficult time for him in the wilderness, but he got around all those stumbling blocks. Things were looking so good. People loved him. We had such good times together. And then..." His voice broke and he paused. "Then he just had to go to Jerusalem. We tried to tell him what would happen, but he wouldn't listen."

He banged his fist upon the table, causing dishes to rattle and a goblet to tip over. "If only he had listened. If only he had not gone to Jerusalem." Peter glanced at Thomas, who nodded in agreement.

Martha automatically moved quickly to wipe up the spill as a youthful voice commented softly, "Didn't the prophets say something about the shepherd being struck down and the sheep being scattered?"[1]

Peter turned to glare, but wasn't sure who had spoken. He presumed it was the young man, Adam, but decided to ignore the remark and return to his pacing.

"Is there anything I can do?" Adam asked as he moved to the table.

"Thanks, Adam," said Martha, "but I think we have it taken care of. There wasn't much of a spill." She smiled at the youth.

Adam, trying to hide his awkwardness, filled his cup and took some cheese and bread. He looked around the room and decided to sit by Andrew for awhile, instead of returning to his parents' side. He offered some of his bread and cheese to Andrew. "Is your brother always this angry and snappish?"

Andrew chuckled. "Not usually so angry, but always quick-tongued. Peter's always been my hero – although I knew I could never be like him. He loved fishing and would have made it his life's work, if Jesus hadn't asked us to follow him. He's quick to react, and I take a long time to think about things, but we both have a passion where Jesus is concerned."

"Were you always a follower of Jesus?" asked Adam. "I mean from the time he started preaching?"

"Well, yes and no," answered Andrew. He paused, pushing back his dark brown hair. It was not unruly like Peter's, but Andrew had picked up the habit from Peter because he wanted to be like him. "We were both fishermen with our father, but I really didn't have the heart for it. I would have joined the Zealots and would probably be dead by now if I hadn't met John the Baptizer. I was one of his followers because..." Andrew paused, smiled and continued, "Well, I guess because that's where the action was."

"You mean the preaching and baptizing?" asked Adam. "I guess that would have been pretty exciting."

"Oh, it was. John didn't waste words or worry about what people thought. Then Jesus came along. Even though we had known Jesus a long time, I sensed something different about him that day. I told Peter I thought Jesus was the Messiah, as well as our friend."

"Did you ever regret leaving John and following Jesus?"

"Oh, sometimes I missed the excitement of John's fiery ways." Andrew laughed softly. "Had I stayed with the Zealots, I might even be leading a rebel band like the one Barabbas led. But I put that all behind me. Jesus' way was quieter, but somehow more powerful. I really believed he was the Messiah, and I tried to follow his example."

Peter's pacing steps strayed from his self-allotted area and moved him to his brother's side. He said nothing, but watched the two as they talked. His brother was much older than the young boy, but much younger than Peter. He always thought of Andrew as a kid. He suddenly realized what a handsome young man Andrew had become.

Andrew, aware of his brother's presence, spoke in a quiet, mellow voice. "I was just telling Adam how we began following Jesus." Peter's flashing dark eyes locked with Andrew's, which were softer and more compassionate. They communicated soul to soul as only brothers who love each other can do. Andrew, keeping his gaze on Peter, continued, "Peter, we all feel the same way you do. We all wish Jesus had not gone to Jerusalem, but he did. We can't go back and change what was. The future is before us, whether we understand it or not. Jesus had to go to Jerusalem. He told us that several times."

Peter grimaced. How did his kid brother become so smart? He blinked and mumbled, "Yeah, I know."

Andrew flashed a sly smile at his brother and winked at Adam. "I'm sure you remember a couple of weeks ago when he told us he was going back to Jerusalem. You called him to task over it. I don't think I will ever forget the look on your face when he called you Satan for your words."[2] Andrew couldn't keep a little chuckle from his voice.

Hot anger flared as Peter faced his brother. He wanted to hold on to that anger, and just rage at something or someone. He didn't want anyone to make him smile, but it was impossible to remain angry, especially with Andrew. Besides that, in his grief he found it difficult to keep his emotions separated one from another. He couldn't hold on to anger – or any other emotion – very long. The twitch at the corner of his mouth pushed a tiny smile across his lips. Before he could stop himself, a slight chuckle escaped his parted lips. Oh, yes, he remembered that day. It was embarrassing, but it was also a memory of the lighter, joyful times mixed with confusion and seriousness.

The men didn't notice the little girl who had joined her brother. Leah loved her brother and she also liked the stories and could sense one coming from these men. "Did Jesus really call you 'Satan'?" Leah's dark eyes seemed even wider than they had earlier.

"Oh, yes," answered Andrew. He didn't mind the child's presence, but he knew Peter's view. Before Peter had a chance to say anything, Andrew winked at Leah. "I'm sure Peter remembers very well."

"How could I forget?" asked Peter in a sarcastic tone, a frown replacing the smile. "You make sure I remember!" Andrew laughed, knowing his brother wasn't really angry.

Peter paused. Ignoring the youth and child and others who listened, he forged ahead. The slight smile returned. His eyes softened as memory took him back to a more care-free time. "It was a beautiful day – not a cloud in the sky. Birds called to one another as if announcing Jesus' presence. We were just enjoying a rare day of joking and having fun. Everything was going so well. Life couldn't get any better. Then, out of the blue, Jesus said, 'I'm going to Jerusalem.'" Peter paused, trying to bring the past more clearly into the present.

He blinked and let the words flow as they would. "I tried to ignore a strange feeling in the pit of my stomach." Peter clutched his stomach, feeling again that nervousness. "I hoped maybe Jesus was just kidding, giving us one of his riddles that he loved so much. I tried to cover my anxiousness by pretending I didn't understand what he was talking about."

"You were outrageous," replied Andrew. "But to be honest, we all agreed with you. We thought surely this was one of his famous riddles or jokes. After all, his life was threatened the last time we had been in Jerusalem."

"Really?" asked Leah.

"Really," said Andrew. "But that didn't stop Jesus."

Peter half-smiled, half-frowned. A tear escaped, trickling down the side of his face. Hastily he brushed it aside. "Since I thought it was all in fun, I was deliberately sarcastic. 'We'll all go with you,' I said. 'Jerusalem is a good city to visit, especially during the festivals – and especially when we're dodging the High Priest's hired head-hunters. We'll play hide-and-seek when we get there. When do we leave?'"

Leah giggled. Adam softly punched her arm.

"It sounds awful now, but I couldn't believe he really wanted to return so soon." Peter paused again, running his hand through his hair. "I tried to pretend I didn't notice the note of sorrow I heard in his voice. He told us he would be killed there, but in three days he would be raised and live again."

Peter once again ran his fingers through his already unruly hair, set his cup on the corner of the table and continued. "Much to my shame, I still ignored the sorrow in his voice and chose to hear what I wanted to hear. I was trying to force us into a happy feeling, and I hoped that he would surely join me. So I blundered on head-long."

"As usual," interrupted Andrew, winking at Adam and Leah. He always enjoyed his brother's rare stories. Peter tried to glare at him, but smiled weakly, shrugged his shoulders and continued.

"Yes, just the way I usually did," Peter answered. "What could I say? He actually said he would be killed. He knew he would die, and yet he was determined to go. I couldn't believe it – or accept it. So I said, 'Wait a minute, Lord. You can't be serious.' I reminded him that we were just getting started together and there was too much to live for. I told him to think of all the hungry people he could feed and all the sick folks who couldn't afford doctors. I reminded him of all the criminals and the crooked, twisted, warped minds that needed his wholeness. Jerusalem could be a fun place, so I suggested that we just go and enjoy the festivals – like a little holiday. He would feel better and all that nonsense about dying would be forgotten."

Peter grimaced as he thought about his next words. He even thought about omitting them from the story, but shrugged his shoulders slightly and continued. "I even reminded him he would soon be in a position to set himself up as King. Then he could rule the world."

"You didn't!" exclaimed John. "I didn't hear you say that."

"Yes," said Peter. "I was really trying to joke like I thought he was. He stopped walking so suddenly I almost ran into him. He stood looking at me like I was crazy or something – like he couldn't believe I had said that. I laughed and said, 'You aren't really going to let them kill you, are you?' I expected him to break into a smile that would tell me he was only kidding. He didn't say a word, only stood there shaking his head. So I asked again, 'You are just joking...aren't you?' Jesus then gave me a strange, sort of sad look. Now I understand that look. I should have known better."

Peter walked to a window where he stared out into the night. Andrew followed. Laying a hand on his shoulder, he said, "Don't be so hard on yourself, brother. How could you have known? How could any of us have known what would happen? We were all thinking what you were willing to say, but we were too afraid to speak. And remember, although he did rebuke you, he called you Pete." Andrew broke into a chuckle that relieved some of the tension. Peter had to smile at his brother. Andrew could always bring joy into the bleakest picture.

"You're right, Andrew," Peter replied. "Sometimes Jesus called me Pete when he was either exasperated or compassionate with me. 'You know, Pete,' he said, 'you're beginning to sound like Satan. He pounded me with those same kind of temptations in the wilderness after John baptized me.' I didn't know then what Jesus was talking about, so he explained some of what Satan said. He told me I was his friend, but I was tempting him to turn away from his journey. Then he told me to get behind him! 'I won't listen to your words of temptation,' he said. 'I must go to Jerusalem. And yes, I will die, but I will also rise again.'"

The words stopped flowing for a minute, and Peter glanced around the room at each person one by one, checking their reactions to his words. No one was laughing at him. There was not even an accusing glance or a raised eyebrow. No one spoke a word. They were all waiting expectantly for the rest of his story.

Feeling a little self-conscious and uncomfortable with those looks of expectation, Peter walked to the table and picked up his cup, which someone filled for him. He took a sip and let it slowly trickle down his throat. It felt as good as it tasted – warming him near his heart which still felt cold within his breast.

Enclosing the cup in his big, rough hands, Peter again began his slow, steady trek of two-step pacing. "I was perplexed, but I certainly couldn't let him go alone, but neither could I let him see how anxious I was – as if he didn't already know."

"Jesus was like that. He always knew more than we thought he did," said one of the women as she continued around the room filling cups for those who wanted it. No one noticed who had spoken. It didn't really matter, since the thought belonged to all of them.

Peter chuckled a little, in spite of his resolve to never laugh again. "I blundered on." He glanced at Andrew to see if he would comment. Andrew grinned and placed his hand over his mouth. Peter frowned at his brother and continued. "I told him I didn't like the idea at all – him going to Jerusalem and dying and all that. I really wondered what would happen to the rest of us. If we went to Jerusalem with him, would we, too, have to give up our lives?

"Jesus looked at me with an expression etched forever in my memory – almost the same look that he had the other night when I..." Peter shook his head to chase away the memory of that moment when the rooster crowed and melted his soul to tears. And even yet, the memory brought unbidden tears to his eyes. Martha tried to cover the brief moment of awkward silence by rattling a few dishes. Peter took a deep breath and once again let the words flow, remembering the joyful times. "'Look, Pete,' Jesus said to me, 'you have to stay in the world for a while. Who do you think is going to spread the word after I'm gone? Why do you think I've spent so much time explaining things to you and the others?'"

Peter, feeling uncomfortable with his confession, as well as with his jovial attitude in a time of grief, could smile because he knew his friend, Jesus, had not taken offense at his words. "It really sounds trivial to me now, but I just couldn't believe he was serious about dying. He was our Messiah! Our King! How could he rule the Kingdom if he died?" Peter again paused, stared out the window into the darkness, trying to see something that wasn't there.

"Like I said before, Peter, don't be so hard on yourself." Andrew knew his brother's tendency to beat up on himself. "We all would have done the same thing if we'd had the opportunity. None of us really believed he meant to die. It didn't make any sense that he should die just when he was getting started and we were beginning to grasp a little of what he was saying to us."

"Only his patience and compassion kept him from walking away from me as he should have done." Peter found his voice a little choked with emotion, but he needed to finish his story. "He placed his arm around my shoulder, and, for the first time since we started that conversation, he sounded like he was joking. It was not a teasing kind of joke. It was more like he was going to play a joke on death itself. He smiled and said, 'But come, my friend. Time is fleeing and I really must get to Jerusalem. Will you come with me?' What could I say? He broke into a brisk walk and I had to run to catch up with him. I tried once more to detain him. He just smiled, shook his head, and kept walking."

Peter slowly walked to the table and set his cup on it and returned to his steady, measured steps. "I tried," he said almost in a whisper. "I tried. Jesus just wouldn't listen. He just would not listen. He kept moving, almost like he was anxious to get there and get it over with."

Peter once again fell into his grief and anger. He turned away from those watching, seeking to hide fresh, unbidden tears. "If only he had listened. If only..."

Chapter Six

Can You See the Wind?

Simon Peter was like a rudderless boat in the Sea of Grief. He understood anger and frustration, which were accompanied by physical slights and encounters, but not grief. Certainly laughter had no place in grief. *How can I laugh one minute and be so angry the next?* Peter's thoughts continued to rage while his feet were confined to a small area where he could only take two or three steps. *I just don't understand anything anymore. Why did Jesus have to die? I was so sure he was the long- awaited Messiah, but I thought the Messiah was supposed to set up a Kingdom like David and make Israel a great nation. So why did he die – and so violently, painfully? He called me Peter the Rock, so why did I melt like lava flowing away from the heat?*

"Is Peter angry because Jesus died?" asked Leah as she turned to her brother.

"Probably, little sister," replied Adam. "He's sad, frustrated and angry all at the same time – angry with himself, with the Romans and the Pharisees who crucified Jesus, and with Jesus for allowing it to happen. He can't take his anger out on the Romans or the Pharisees. They would strike back. And certainly he can't attack Jesus, so that only leaves himself – and his friends."

Hearing Adam's response, James thought, *The boy has pretty sharp perception for a youth.* He was about to comment to Adam when Peter turned abruptly to face Nicodemus and Joseph of Arimathea, who were sitting on low stools, talking quietly together. Their words could not be heard, but Nicodemus suddenly dropped his face into his hands, and his body shook with grief.

Sensing Peter's determined stare, Nicodemus lifted his tear-streaked face. Peter, still feeling somewhat embarrassed by his own confession, tried to avert the attention from himself and quench the new flare of burning anger within his heart. He hurled an angry accusation at the two men. Pointing to them with an accusing finger, he raised his voice, which cracked with emotion. "Your clothes look like you are from the Sanhedrin. So, why are you here? You aren't his followers. Were you there at Golgotha? Did you see and hear what happened to Jesus?"

Even before they answered, Peter knew they were there. He saw them. But he had to say something. He had to vent his anger and frustration on someone – and hopefully, no one had seen him hiding in the brush.

The air fairly crackled with tension. Peter was impetuous and sometimes explosive. The little band of grieving friends could not afford to have trouble which would bring the Roman soldiers running to the house. Thomas paled and started for the door. Joseph opened his mouth to speak, but Nicodemus, laying a hand on his friend's arm, raised the other in caution. Then Nicodemus sat quietly, eyes locked with Peter's glare for such a long time the others thought maybe he was just going to ignore the angry questions. Peter blinked, opened his mouth to speak, but closed it without a word.

Finally Nicodemus spoke quietly. "Yes, Peter, Joseph and I were there. We saw and we heard it all. Why are we here? I'm not sure I really know. Of course, I can only speak for myself, not for Joseph. Perhaps I am trying to give comfort to each one of you, but I suspect I'm just trying to absorb more comfort for myself from you. Possibly I am just trying to recapture the past, find a direction for my life, and learn a little more about Jesus in the process."

Joseph nodded. "Yes," he added, "we're here simply because we believed him and hope to gain some comfort."

Nicodemus didn't turn his gaze from Peter, nor did Peter back down. Nicodemus spoke clearly and without wavering. "You see, my walk with Jesus started sometime back. It's true I am a member of the Sanhedrin. Maybe you're right to question my reason for being here with you this night. I'm not really a part of your group. And yet..." His voice trailed away as he finally lowered his gaze.

Peter shifted uncomfortably from one foot to the other. He really hadn't expected an answer, and now he wasn't sure what to do with it. Nicodemus regained his composure and began to speak once again more clearly. "Let me tell my story and then you can be the judge."

Nicodemus was different from the others. He was not a big man, and his beard hung to his chest, an indication of his age. His brow was permanently creased by age and by many decisions wrought with anxiety. His eyes, however, were not the cold, calculating eyes usually associated with the Sanhedrin. They were soft and compassionate – and wet. Nicodemus was not ashamed of his tears.

Peter felt rooted to the spot, unable to take his eyes from Nicodemus. It was hard to believe a member of the Sanhedrin was really in their midst. But then, Peter was finding a lot of things hard to believe. He sensed the others watching him, wondering if he would try to stop Nicodemus from talking. What could he do? It really wasn't his choice.

Nicodemus took Peter's silence as consent and began to speak slowly, deliberately. "My name is Nicodemus – as most of you already know." Every eye turned toward him. Every ear tuned to his words. The tension slowly faded and people began to relax, wanting to hear yet another story of Jesus added to their treasure house of who he was.

"I attended the best schools and my education is envied by many." The words did not sound arrogant or full of pride. He was simply stating the facts. "In the Sanhedrin, we only have token authority. Once we had real power, now we have none. In some of the religious areas we're allowed to rule, and yet we must always answer to Rome. All my life I have tried to keep an open mind. The Law is firm, but I believe in it. It's our way of life. I believe in the God of Abraham and Sarah, of Isaac and Rebecca – of Jacob, who was named Israel. God led Israel from Egypt to the Promised Land, through captivity, and beyond – even to this day. The Torah tells us that a Messiah was promised. God is a God of love and mercy, as well as a God of justice and judgment. All my life I believed, but all my life I also questioned. I wondered about the Messiah. When would he come? How would we know him?"

Anger drained from Peter as quickly as it had flared. He relaxed and listened with the rest. Deep in his heart he knew they needed to hear as much about Jesus as they could. He locked his hands together behind his back and leaned against the door for support. The soft voice of Nicodemus soothed the tension in his overwrought nerves.

The midnight hour had come and gone, and the friends were determined to stay awake for the night. Several of the women began once again quietly making the rounds – pouring drinks and offering bread and cheese. John once more moved to Mary's side, making sure she was all right. Leah leaned against her mother, dozing. Others settled back, some even closing their eyes, as they listened to yet another side of Jesus.

Nicodemus, if not fully accepted, was at least politely respected. "One day I heard about the man from Nazareth. Some of my colleagues called him an ignorant upstart. They said he left carpentry for preaching. I was curious and interested. How could anyone who is unlearned say and do the things they said he was doing? He was an unusual person, but throughout our history God sent unusual persons to us in our time of need.

"Most of my colleagues in the Sanhedrin didn't understand my desire to hear Jesus. They thought he should be locked away where he wouldn't be a threat to them. But all those stories about blind people being able to see and lame people throwing away their crutches...Well, I had to see for myself."

Joshua smiled to himself, unconsciously brushing his hand across his eyes. "A lot of people were confused when folks were healed. Our world can't stand beggars who can't see, but they don't know what to do with them when they are healed."

Nicodemus glanced at the man and nodded. "You're right, my friend. When a person's status changes, we have to change the way we think about him. It is easier to throw a few coins than to welcome them into our fellowship of friends."

Joshua smiled again. "None of that mattered to Jesus. Blind or clear sight, lame or active, he loved us all."

Nicodemus looked at the man curiously. "You sound like a man with a story to tell yourself."

Joshua grinned. "Yes, I do, but first we'll hear yours. It looks like Jesus touched folks from the richest to the poorest. Please continue."

Nicodemus closed his eyes in thought for a minute. "Jesus was a master storyteller and teacher, but I don't need to tell you that."

Leah, dozing with her head on her mother's lap, roused, stretched and yawned. Hearing his words in her half-sleep state, she remarked, "Yeah, he told great stories when we could get him away from the big people."

Everyone laughed at the unexpected response. Leah opened her eyes in surprise. Her mother pushed her head back to her lap and said, "Hush. Go back to sleep."

Nicodemus chuckled and resumed his story. "Jesus spoke with an authority that was unequaled among any of the scribes, priests or rabbis that I knew. And yet, they said he ate with sinners and talked to women with questionable reputations."

The Samaritan woman, taking a break from serving, stood alone beside a window, watching and listening. She coughed softly, cleared her throat, and remarked with a hint of sarcasm, "Questionable women? How strange."

Nicodemus surprised by her response, glanced at her and then chuckled. He knew she was from Samaria, and although he didn't know her story, he was sure she had one to tell. "That's what we were told," he said, smiling at her.

She bowed to him in mock submission and leaned back against the wall to listen to his story. She liked the strange little man from the Sanhedrin. He was different – like herself.

Nicodemus continued, unconsciously folding and unfolding the pleats of his robe as he talked. "I was curious, so I decided I must see him in action and talk to him if I could. My sources told me he spent much time alone in a garden during the evening hours – talking to himself, they said. They had no idea that he might be praying. For them prayer was for others to hear, to exhibit righteousness."

"What are sources?" asked Leah. Drifting in and out of sleep, she didn't miss much. She noticed no difference between Nicodemus and the others people there, except she thought his clothes were pretty.

Nicodemus smiled at the little girl. "Sources are a who, not a what – at least for me they were. They were people who found out where Jesus was and what he was doing. Then they gave me the information."

"Oh, you mean they were spies," she said as understanding spread across her face.

Adam looked for a place to hide. "Leah! You don't call people in the employment of the Sanhedrin spies."

"That's what they were, weren't they, Mr. Nicodemus?"

Andrew laughed, and others tried to hide embarrassed giggles. "She's right, you know," he said. "It looks like someone is going to keep us honest and out in the open tonight." And he threw back his head and laughed heartily again.

Nicodemus laughed, too. "You are right, Andrew. Yes, if we're honest, source is a fancy name for spy."

He thought for a minute while the rest began to relax more. The child was certainly keeping them from dwelling on their grief.

"Anyway," he continued with his story, "they told me the garden was at the edge of town. Although I'd never been there, I knew where it was. They told me he went there late at night while everyone else was sleeping. I really wanted to talk to him, and since I wasn't too eager for anyone to know it, a lonely garden, late at night was fine with me.

"Making sure I wasn't followed," he spoke in a mysterious tone of voice for Leah's sake, "I went to the garden.[1] It really was more of a courtyard – a quiet place with stone benches, trees and flowers. It was a good place to hide or retreat, especially at night. The sky was full of stars sparkling more brilliantly than I ever saw them. I had no need of a torch, since the moon filled the night with light. When I got there, a charcoal fire was burning in a circle of stones – not a large blazing fire, just enough for warming the hands to take the chill off.

"I saw him sitting alone, so motionless he could have been a statue. He turned and indicated for me to join him, almost as if he expected me. I greeted him and told him who I was. Somehow I felt he already knew who I was and why I was there. However, I felt I needed an excuse for being there, so I pretended I had just gone out for a stroll. I tried a little small talk about the weather."

There was a chuckle from Nathaniel, who stepped to the table to fill his cup and take a snack. "My guess is he didn't stick with the weather bit very long. Knowing Jesus, he probably said something like, 'I know who you are. I saw you while you were hiding behind the curtains watching me.'"

Nicodemus' whole body shook with laughter. "You are right, Nathaniel. Jesus said, 'I know who you are, Nicodemus. I have been waiting for you.' I wondered how he knew who I was, or that I would be there. I didn't know for sure myself until I knew where he was. I wasn't about to press the issue, so I let it slide."

"Good thinking," replied Nathaniel. Most of them knew Nathaniel.[2] He was under a tree when Philip called him to come with him to meet the man from Nazareth. His comment was, "Can anything good come out of Nazareth?" Of course Jesus told him what he said and where he was when he said it. Nathaniel knew from experience that Jesus went directly to the heart of any matter.

Nicodemus nodded and smiled. "I tried a different approach. I tried to pretend that the rest of the Sanhedrin had sent me."

"Not a good idea," said Nathaniel, shaking his head. He chuckled softly and took his snack back to his seat.

"You're right again, my friend," laughed Nicodemus. "Clearing my throat to stop the nervous quiver in my voice, I said, 'Rabbi, we know you are a teacher of God. You couldn't do the things you do if you weren't.' I wanted him to think I was knowledgeable about him and maybe even a follower. Logic told me if I said I believed he was a good teacher, that should flatter him and put me in good standing."

Nathaniel chuckled again, and Nicodemus smiled. Others joined them. They could see Nicodemus was backing himself into the proverbial corner.

"Well, obviously I didn't receive the compliment I had hoped for," Nicodemus laughed. "I wanted to hear him say, 'That's good, Nicodemus. It's important to believe.' But he didn't say that. Instead, he said, 'Nicodemus, it's good that you believe, but unless you are born again, you cannot see God's kingdom.'" Nicodemus paused.

"I never heard such teachings before! I've read everything in the law. I know it inside and out, from front to back and back to front. I believed myself to be an intelligent man, but at that moment, I felt absolutely ignorant. I had no idea on earth what he was talking about."

Nicodemus shifted in his seat, reached for his cup and took a sip. "I was beginning to think I shouldn't have come, but I was there so I plunged on like I knew what I was talking about. I told him I didn't understand. I said, 'I'm an old man. Can I go back into my mother's womb and start all over again?'"

There was a quiet ripple of chuckling and snickering around the room.

"That sounded really stupid, didn't it? I knew better. A person cannot be physically born again. I guess I hoped maybe that man of miracles could somehow turn back the hands of time and give me a chance to live my life over.

"He didn't ridicule my ignorance. He simply explained the difference between being born physically and spiritually. While he spoke, I remembered how the prophet Ezekiel said God will give a new heart and a new spirit. He will take out the heart of stone and give me a new heart of flesh.[3]

"Suddenly things began to make sense to me. Jesus was asking me to become a new kind of person. I knew he was right, of course. In order to change I would have to get rid of some undesirable habits and attitudes. No one ever told me that quite the way Jesus did. I could almost feel the cold, stony heart within my breast and could not stop the shiver that ran from my head to my toes."

Nicodemus shivered slightly even as he remembered that night in the garden with Jesus. Had a breeze blown through the open window? Or was it only the remembrance? Or maybe the Spirit? Nicodemus hurried on with his story, hoping no one noticed the tremble in his voice.

"I tried to be nonchalant, but it was as if Jesus could see right through me. He asked why it surprised me he would say I must be born again. I had a smart remark on the tip of my tongue, but I closed my mouth without speaking." Nicodemus paused and glanced at Nathaniel, who was nodding and smiling.

"You learn fast, my friend," said Nathaniel.

Nicodemus laughed and continued. "I glanced up at the stars and remembered God's promise to Abraham.[4] We sat in silence enjoying the beauty of the night, watching a soft breeze make the leaves dance. The breeze played tag with the embers, causing a small blaze to shoot up, desperately trying to rekindle a fire. It soon died away, leaving only the glowing coals. We had been quiet for so long I was startled me when he spoke. 'Look, Nicodemus,' he said. 'Did you see that wind?'"

Nicodemus paused and glanced around the room. He smiled at the look of awe and confusion on that sea of faces. "I must have looked as confused as I felt, because he chuckled as he continued, 'You heard its sound. You saw what it did to the coals, but did you actually see the wind?' Of course, I could only sit there feeling dumb. No one can see wind. I knew he must have a point to make, so I waited quietly. He continued, 'That is the way of the Spirit and everyone who is born of the Spirit.'

"I was getting more confused. He spoke of the wind and the Spirit almost as if they were one. I wasn't sure which he really meant. Would the Spirit of God fan the flames within the heart of a person? Could being born again and the wind/spirit be somehow related?"

"That sure sounds like one of his riddles," said Peter, who was fascinated by this man's story in spite of himself.

"'How could that be?' I asked." Nicodemus smiled at Peter. "It was sort of like when he called you Satan, Peter. He smiled, and with a note of surprise in his voice, said, 'Why, Nicodemus! I am surprised at you! Can it be that you are a teacher of Israel and do not know these things? When I talk about simple earthly things like the wind and you do not understand, how do you expect to understand things like the Spirit of God, rebirth and Kingdom?'"

Peter nodded and smiled grudgingly at this little man from the Sanhedrin, who seemed so much out of place. He could actually understand how Nicodemus must have felt. He could imagine Jesus sitting in that sheltered garden, teasing Nicodemus with these deep theological riddles.

Nicodemus continued, "We talked the rest of the night. He told me God loved me so much he sent his own Son to earth. He really understood my dilemma. As a trained lawyer of the Sanhedrin, I was obligated to follow the Law of Moses, and yet, I needed to know more about being born again. I wanted my life to mean something to someone else."

Nicodemus paused and glanced toward the window, looking for a dawn that was only in his memory. "The first rays of the morning's sun began to spread the sky with streaks of red and yellow, and he talked about light in darkness. He said he was the true light which could lead me, and others like me, through the darkness sin had created in God's universe. We heard street vendors preparing for business as we separated. Jesus gave me so much to think about, but I had a full day ahead of me, and I knew he did also."

Nicodemus paused, expecting a question or comment from Leah, but she was leaning against her mother, sleeping as only a child can sleep – looking like one of the cherubs of God.

Closing his eyes, Nicodemus tried to keep the picture of that night clear in his mind. He opened his eyes and shook his head sadly. "I didn't get a chance to talk with him again after that night. Some time later a few of my colleagues heard him proclaim to be the answer to our Scriptures. They were visibly upset and came into the council room fuming, asking how they could get rid of that poor carpenter who thought he was a rabbi. As you well know, many people were beginning to believe he was the Christ, or at least a prophet. The temple police wanted to arrest him, but were afraid of causing a riot, so they came back to the council complaining to us about him stirring up the people, wondering what we could, or would, do about it.[5]

"Caiaphas asked them why they didn't arrest him when they had the opportunity. The police said they had never heard anyone speak like that before. Some Pharisees accused them of being deceived, also. I could not keep from smiling to myself as they spoke. Remembering the wind blowing where it will and we cannot stop it, I had learned how difficult it was to argue with him. Even now, every time I feel a breeze, I hear his words and know the Spirit of God is there." Nicodemus glanced at Nathaniel and smiled.

"The Council wanted to crucify him. They couldn't tolerate anyone who said things they didn't understand. My life had been changed because of him, so I had to at least try to help him. It was a feeble attempt, but I asked them if our law judges a person without first giving a hearing. They turned and glared daggers at me so sharp I could almost feel them pierce my heart. They asked if I was one of Jesus' followers and if I had also come from Galilee. 'What do you know about him?' they sneered at me." Nicodemus curled his mouth and wrinkled his nose and did a weak imitation of the High Priest who had rebuked him.

Leah chose that moment to rouse from napping on her mother's lap. She giggled. "Did he really sound like that?" she asked.

"Oh, worse, little one, much worse," he answered her as seriously as he could. It was difficult to keep a straight face when talking with Leah. She seemed to pull the child from deep within the most proper adult.

"What did you do?" she asked just as seriously.

"Since I couldn't defend my own mixed emotions, I could say no more in the defense of Jesus. They really didn't expect an answer anyway. I'm ashamed and filled with remorse, but I'm such a babe in the faith. You see, Leah, new birth in the Spirit is like a new baby in the house. When you were born, you were helpless and depended on those who loved you to feed and nourish you. Then you got a little older, and now you can do many things, but you still don't have all the ability and understanding of an adult. I'm growing, but I was, and still am, so young in the faith."

Nicodemus paused to collect his thoughts as others remembered how they were changed and how many times they also failed him. "I was so very busy. There were a lot of people in town and I had so many questions to answer. It was impossible for me to keep up with his itinerary. I couldn't ask very often of his whereabouts without arousing suspicion. But I wanted to hear him – to talk with him again."

"Where were your...sources?" Leah asked with satisfaction at remembering the word.

"They were more interested in finding something false to report to the Pharisees. I couldn't trust them anymore."

"Well, that's the way it is with spies," Leah stated as if she had revealed some great truth.

Nicodemus couldn't hide his smile. James and Nathaniel chuckled. Adam turned away so his sister wouldn't see him smile. Even Peter turned abruptly to stare out the window. The child was outrageous, but she was right. His smile faded as Nicodemus continued his story. "Before I had another opportunity to find Jesus and talk with him, business took me out of town for a few days. When I returned, the first thing I heard was news of his trial – if you could call it a trial. I couldn't believe they really did it, and so quickly. I rushed immediately to Golgotha, but I was too late."

Nicodemus paused, wiped his eyes, took a deep breath and moved toward the conclusion of his story. "If only I had been here, maybe..." The words trailed off. Then quietly, almost in a whisper, forgetting the others were listening, Nicodemus mused, "Would I have been too timid, or too fearful, to stand up to the rest of the Sanhedrin? I wish I could say that I would have spoken out, but I don't know. I just don't know."

Mary turned from gazing out the window. "You could have done nothing to prevent it, Nicodemus. Don't blame yourself. It was the road he chose to fulfill the promise."

Nicodemus felt the tension begin to drain from his taut nerves and muscles. Mary's compassion for his feelings gave him courage to finish his story. Glancing at Joseph of Arimathea, who had been listening from the door to the garden, Nicodemus nodded and continued. "When Joseph from Arimathea asked for his body, I went with him. Mixing myrrh and aloes, we anointed his body, then wrapped him in linen cloths and placed him in the tomb in the garden until after the Day of Preparation. We will go with you when the sun rises and finish the job."[6]

Nicodemus fixed his gaze upon Peter, who stared back like one caught in the hypnotic trance of the cobra's stare. "Yes, Peter, I was there. I did see them crucify my Lord. I felt the darkness, and the earth shake. I shivered again, as I did that night so long ago in the garden when that little breeze stirred up the coals. The Wind – the Spirit of God – blows where it will. It cannot be stopped by killing a body."

"You're right, my friend." It was Lazarus who spoke.

His story finished, Nicodemus dropped his gaze, sat back in his chair, buried his face in his hands. He would wait for the dawn. And then...

Chapter Seven

Water and Truth

The words of Nicodemus faded, and soft murmurs rose and fell once again, filling the gap. Peter, however, stood like a statue, hardly breathing. He felt caught in a hypnotic trance. Unsuccessfully, he tried to sort his feelings. Grief with all its mixture of emotions was foreign to him. All those emotions – love, hate, anger, joy, peace – seemed to wrestle and struggle for top priority. He was filled with anger – or was it jealousy? – that an outsider like Nicodemus could know Jesus so well. At the same time, he felt a sense of kinship and awe for the courage, as well as the lack of courage, in Nicodemus. Peter struggled to harness his emotions and gain control. Blinking, he released the spell of the trance-like stare and tried to move a little more around the room.

As he neared the corner where the Samaritan woman was sitting, a muffled sob from her caught his attention. Peter stopped in his tracks, facing the woman. *I don't want to share my grief with outsiders – and especially a Samaritan woman*, he thought.

Sensing Peter's eyes upon her, the woman raised head and brushed her hand across her tear-streaked face. Compassion almost caught him, but Peter forced it aside, giving an edge to his voice. "Who are you and why are you here? You're certainly not one of us. And besides that, you're a woman."

It was an obvious observation. Martha, about to fill a cup for one of the disciples, turned and stared at Peter in disbelief, the pitcher paused above the cup. Mary, her sister, also turned and stared at him with eyes wide and mouth open. Even Mary, the Mother of Jesus, and the other women in the room turned to him with questioning looks. Peter, more than a little disconcerted, tried to amend his statement. "Well, a Samaritan woman," he stammered. He knew that didn't help the situation any, so he had to take his foot out of his mouth and begin again. By this time the sharpness of his voice had lost its edge.

"All right, I'm sorry," he said, facing Martha and throwing his hands up in defeat. "I know Jesus would not have allowed that kind of prejudice. You women have been very important in our work."

Turning back to the Samaritan woman, he tried to ease his frustration. With the sharpness gone from his voice, he spoke barely above a whisper. "I guess I really have no right anyway, but...well... I know I've seen you before. Obviously you're from Samaria, so who are you and why are you with us tonight?" His tone sounded more confused than angry.

The woman took a deep breath. Trying to appear calm, her bright eyes continued to focus on Peter's confused ones. There was a slight quiver in her voice, but she held firm to her inner resolve. She knew she was one of the mourners, and with or without Peter's approval she would stay the night.

"You're right, Simon Peter." She spoke softly, but with conviction. "I am different from you, and as you say, I'm a Samaritan. Normally we would have no more to do with Jews than you would with us, but what is normal anymore?"

She lowered her gaze from Peter's flashing, angry eyes and glanced around the room. "You saw me in Samaria. My name is Sarah – at least that's the name I chose when Jesus gave me a new life. I was there at the cross and saw the soldiers place Jesus on it. The sound of that hammer striking the nails still rings in my ears."

Sarah lifted her hands to cover her ears and squeezed her eyes shut. She could no more turn off the memory than she could have stopped the sound at the cross. Peter could not move. He didn't expect her to answer. Certainly he would never be interested in anything a Samaritan woman would have to say! However, he was unexpectedly drawn into the courage of this woman who defied custom to be with

Jesus at the end. He should have been at his side, and wasn't.

Taking another deep breath and slowly exhaling, Sarah glanced at Peter, who continued to watch her with curiosity. She rubbed her hands together, as one would rub away pain. Then holding them before her, almost as if she expected to see the holes and the blood dripping from them, the Samaritan woman spoke with a slight catch in her voice. "I even felt the pain of those nails."

She bowed her head and a shudder rippled over her. The already quiet room became even more hushed as the rest waited for her to either continue her story or back away from Peter's angry stare. Peter's arm twitched slightly, almost reaching out to her in compassion, but she lifted her head, shrugged her shoulders helplessly, took another deep breath, and continued. Peter pulled his arm back to his side.

"Why am I here?" she repeated Peter's question. "Like Nicodemus, I'm not sure. I just didn't want to be alone tonight. I need companionship with others who loved him as I did. My heart is breaking, as I'm sure each of yours is. Maybe if I tell my story, it will ease my pain and help me remember."

Peter glared for a moment, not sure what to say. How could he back down gracefully? The other women warned him with a look that penetrated his soul. Andrew once again stood beside his brother. With a hand on Peter's arm, he urged Peter to listen to Sarah. "Let's hear her story. I'm sure you remember her talking to Jesus at the Well of Jacob."[1] Andrew usually could get his brother's attention with his soft-spoken persuasion when others could not. For a brief moment their eyes met, each trying to read the other's thoughts.

Andrew knew his brother remembered the day, but he continued anyway. "We were on our way back to Galilee. Jesus just had to go through Samaria, even though we would have preferred the longer way home. When we got to Jacob's Well, he said he wanted to rest there awhile and sent us on ahead to find food. When we returned, she was there at the well with him."

Peter frowned. "How could I forget?" Rubbing his hand across his face, he tried to blot the scene from his memory – or maybe bring it more clearly into focus. Even he was not sure which.

Leah stretched and yawned, making a low, groaning sound. Surprised by the sound, Peter turned toward her. "Samaria is a long way off, isn't it?" she asked.

"Well, yes it is," answered the Samaritan woman, smiling to herself, glad for the diversion.

"Then how did you get here?" Leah asked as she stretched again.

"Leah, that's none of your business," said Adam. "Don't pay any attention to her," he said to the woman. "She should be sleeping." He turned and scowled at his sister.

The woman's smile turned to laughter – a soft bubbly sound. "Oh, it's all right," she said. "It is a long way and I guess I came by foot most of the way. Can I tell you how I met Jesus and why it was important for me to come to Jerusalem?"

Peter shrugged and nodded to the woman. The unfamiliar feeling of embarrassment was overshadowed by his curiosity. The picture of Jesus by the well talking to the woman was clear in his mind. He really wanted to know more.

Andrew glanced at John, who nodded his approval. Around the room others also nodded approval. "We need to hear all the stories we can to keep the memory of Jesus alive," he said. "Then we'll be able to pass the Word to our children and our children's children. Tell us your story." Andrew squeezed his brother's arm and smiled at Sarah

Grudgingly, Peter knew Andrew was right. He knew he had no right to stop her. He glanced at John, who smiled as if he had read Peter's thoughts. Peter shrugged his shoulders again and returned to the corner once again for his slow two-step back and forth pacing. The Samaritan woman began her story with the determination of one who had news too wonderful to keep to oneself.

"Andrew is right. I did meet Jesus that day at the Well of Jacob. I was called many names, none of them worth repeating, but now I call myself Sarah because Jesus filled me with new life and laughter."

Sarah stood and slowly walked to the table to fill her cup. She was not a young woman, but neither did she look old, despite the hard life she had lived. Dark hair sporting streaks of gray hung around her shoulders. She wore a dress – or rather a tunic – of dark green or gray. In the candlelight it was hard to tell which. A wide red sash held it in at the waist. Sarah would not be considered beautiful, but was pleasing to look upon. And when she chose to smile, which she did quite often since meeting Jesus, her whole face reflected her joy. Sarah's once-hard features softened as she knit her brow in thought. She wanted to encourage others to tell their stories the way she had received encouragement from Nicodemus.

She returned to her chair. "Sychar, a little village on the edge of Samaria, is my home. About noon every day I went to Jacob's Well to draw water."

She turned to Andrew. "The day you're referring to was a scorching hot day. I can almost feel the heat as I remember it. I neared the well and saw a man sitting on the edge of it. He looked very tired and weary, but he had nothing to lower into the well for water. No one else was in sight and I wondered why he was alone. It's not safe for anyone – man or woman – to travel alone in that section of our country.

"Anyway, when I reached the well, he asked me for a drink of water. I knew he must be awfully thirsty, but he was a Jew and I was a Samaritan. I assumed that he was a rabbi, and I was only a woman." Sarah could not help tossing a glance toward Peter, who grimaced and turned away from her gaze as she emphasized the word *only*.

"I was a little angry that he would even speak to me, much less ask me to draw water for him. I reminded him he was a Jew and I a Samaritan woman. I was sure he understood the customs, but I also reminded him Jews and Samaritans don't speak to each other and men don't talk to women."

A smile spread across her face. "How foolish of me! Of course Jesus knew he was a rabbi and I a woman. I guess I was a little like Nicodemus when he pretended the Sanhedrin had sent him to the garden."

Nicodemus nodded and returned her smile. "There was nothing Jesus didn't already know," he said. She agreed.

Sarah paused, frowning. "His words were confusing to me, however. It seemed he was saying one thing when he meant something else. It was like the spirit/wind that baffled Nicodemus." Sarah's eyes met those of Nicodemus, who smiled and nodded to her. He understood her confusion.

"Jesus said if I really knew who I was talking to, I would have asked for Living Water and he would have given it to me. I felt even more bewildered. Jacob's Well is very deep, but does not contain living water."

"What is living water?" asked Leah, wrinkling her nose. "I didn't know water could be alive."

Sarah laughed. "It is called living because it moves – sort of like an underground river."

"Oh. What kind of water was in the well? Dead water?"

"Leah!" Adam was exasperated with his little sister as smothered laughs could be heard around the room. He really wanted to know the difference himself, but he couldn't ask. He was too old.

Sarah smiled at them and all around the room were gasps, giggles, coughs, and smiles. "No, it's not called dead water, although it comes from deep within the ground and sometimes tastes stale and stagnant. I knew there was no running water anywhere near Jacob's Well, so how could Jesus offer me living water?"

Remembering her next words, Sarah laughed a soft little chuckle. "I asked him what on earth he was talking about. He didn't even have anything for drawing water. Jacob's Well was very deep and had been around for centuries, so I asked him if he thought he was greater than our father Jacob, who dug the well, or if he thought he could produce a spring of running water where Jacob could not. He avoided my angry questions and answered me with more confusing words."

"Jesus always loved riddles and word games," said John. "I'm sure he enjoyed every minute with you."

"I'm sure he did, and I did too. No one ever really gave me credit for having a mind before and being able to understand things." The memory brought another quick smile to her face.

Peter stopped pacing and stood motionless, staring at her. He was really beginning to understand this woman, and that worried him. He also knew what it was like to be on the receiving end of those confusing words. How often he had said, "Lord, I don't understand. Explain that to me."

Sarah saw his surprised look. Understanding Peter's perplexed stare, she chose not to make any comment about it and continued with her story. "Jesus told me anyone who would drink from that, or any other well, would get thirsty again in a few hours, but anyone who would drink the water he offered would never thirst again. He offered a spring of eternal, living water found within the soul.

"I was so dense. Perhaps it was because of my anger. Maybe my life was so overshadowed by the past I simply couldn't understand. But of one thing I was certain. It sounded like I would never have to come out in the heat of the day and draw water again. I wanted whatever he offered." Sarah paused, sipping thoughtfully from the cup she held firmly in her hands.

Leah stretched and yawned again. Looking up at her mother, she asked, "Why didn't she go to the well in the evening or morning when it was cool with the other women?"

An embarrassed silence was followed by her mother's hoarse whisper, "Shhh. Go back to sleep."

"But I want to know why..." the persistent child began. She paused when she noticed the silence and everyone looking at her. "Besides, all this talk about water is making me thirsty." She squirmed to get down. Her mother held her tightly.

"Just be quiet, will you?" said her exasperated brother. He stood and moved toward the table. "I'll get you a drink of water."

Adam walked quickly to the table and took a cup of water for the child. Pausing beside Sarah, he apologized. "Please excuse my little sister. She doesn't understand."

Sarah smiled at the young man and turned to the child to explain. "Someday you'll understand," she said, wishing with all her heart it would be possible for the child to be spared such knowledge. "My life was...well, different. I couldn't go with the rest of the women."

"You mean you were a night woman," stated the little girl in her matter-of-fact way. Her dark eyes sparkled in the reflected light of flickering candles.

"Leah!" The young man's already red face turned a brighter scarlet. He hurried to his sister with the glass of water, not sure if he would give it to her to drink or pour it over her head. Her mother gasped and tried to hide her humiliation.

Spontaneous laughter exploded from Sarah, which gave her face a special glow. "Children know a lot more than we give them credit for knowing, don't they?" She stood, slowly walked toward Leah, and laid a hand lovingly on the child's cheek. "Yes, Leah, I was a night woman. I wasn't allowed to go to the well with the rest of the women."

"I bet Jesus didn't care," said Leah with all the wisdom of a six-year-old who is secure in her knowledge. "Jesus didn't care what people did. He loved everyone."

"You're right, Leah," replied Sarah, smiling indulgently at her. She returned to her chair and resumed her story. "Even as I asked him for the water, I sensed that he was talking about something far deeper than Jacob's Well. It seemed almost as if he was saying that within a person is a deep well, fed by the Living Water which springs from God himself. It is that spring of Living Water which satisfies our thirst for God. A beautiful, warm feeling came over me as I thought about his words. A new feeling of hope was taking the place of the despair that had been so much a part of me. I wondered if my life could really change. His next words startled me back to reality. Can you imagine my dismay when he asked me to call my husband so we could talk more? I knew our custom. Men talk of religious things so they can explain to women, but I fell with a jarring thud from hope to the pit of despair.

"I was beginning to feel very uncomfortable. Even though I wanted to hear more about the Living Water, I was at a loss as to what I should do. Surely he knew the kind of life I lived. I couldn't understand why he was talking to me at all. I became more confused and flustered."

Pausing, Sarah took a drink from her cup as she replayed the scene in her memory. No one hurried her. She struggled, trying to decide how much to reveal of herself. Others were also lost in thought. Sarah continued her story, a look of resolve on her face. She would be completely honest with these friends of Jesus.

"I sort of lied to him, I guess," she said, not sure how they would receive her honesty. No one made light of it. They all understood. Receiving courage from their attentiveness, Sarah was able to sort out the truth. "I told him that I wasn't married and didn't have a husband. It was truth, as far as it went. I was so thirsty for that Living Water he offered, I thought if I didn't have a husband, he would continue to teach me.

"Of course he knew. He caught me off guard again when he said, 'You're right. You have no husband – now. You've had five husbands and the man in your home is not your husband. You have indeed spoken the truth.'"

Sarah dropped her head to hide her embarrassment and shame. She was not sure she could continue her story. Tears came unbidden. She would have fled the house to the dark streets of Jerusalem had she not felt someone's arms around her. She raised her head to see Martha smiling at her. "It's all right," Martha spoke with compassion. "Jesus once said, 'Let anyone who has not sinned throw the first stone.'[2] We have all sinned in our own way. The important thing is that you live a forgiven life, or you would not be with us tonight. Take your time and we'll hear more of your story when you're ready."

Mary, surprised by Martha's words, glanced at their brother Lazarus with raised eyebrows. Was this their sister who was always the worker, thinking and talking of spiritual matters? Hope was abounding that night! Lazarus winked at Mary, guessing her thoughts. Gratefully Sarah received Martha's ministry of love, and through the tears that still flowed, she tried to smile as she said, "Thank you, Martha. Yes, I must continue. It's important for me to finish my story."

Martha stood close to her with her hand on Sarah's shoulder until the Samaritan woman sighed deeply and words began to flow once more. Martha then moved on to care for the comfort of others.

"I couldn't look him in the eyes. I felt so alone...so...so miserable. I thought maybe if I changed the subject, I would be able to shake the turmoil and churning in the pit of my stomach. Clearing my throat, I tried to make my voice sound normal. I told him that he sounded like a prophet of some kind."

Again the memory brought a fleeting smile. "That was stupid, wasn't it?" she said as she glanced at Nathaniel. "Of course, he was a prophet of some kind – and much more – to be able to tell me all he had told me."

Nathaniel smiled and shook his head. "It is amazing how much we tried to be self-sufficient and know-it-all, when all the time Jesus was a step – or more – ahead of us."

The others laughed softly with her and Nathaniel at their own foolishness to think Jesus could be deterred from his goal. Even Peter could not keep the smile, however momentary, from his face.

The smile continued to play at the corners of Sarah's eyes, giving them a sparkle. "He smiled at me. I determined to change the subject away from me, so I moved to a safer subject, one which had been debated for centuries. I brought up the old feud about worshipping on the mountain versus worshipping in Jerusalem."

There was a slight groan all around the room. Sarah nodded in agreement. "I know. Everyone knows the argument. It's been discussed for so long there could possibly be nothing new to say about it. Even I would not have approached it, if I had not been desperate."

"I don't know about the argument," said Leah, looking at her mother imploringly. "What was it about?"

"Later, Leah," her mother said quietly.

"But I want to know now," she said with a pout.

"It goes back hundreds of years, Leah," said Adam. "The Samaritans said the mountain in Samaria is the place closest to God. The Jews said the temple in Jerusalem was the place. Now be quiet so we can hear the rest of Sarah's story."

"Well, all right, if you promise to tell me more later."

"I will," said her brother, who loved his sister very much, even when she embarrassed and irritated him.

Sarah smiled at them and then continued. "I thought that would be a safe enough argument. After all, as Adam said, Samaritans and Jews have disputed over it so long no one really knows for sure when or how it even began. I knew all about my religion and about the Messiah who was to come, but still something was missing.

"Again he surprised me. He said, 'Someday neither the mountain nor Jerusalem will be the place to worship.' Then he told me while salvation is from the Jews, true worshipers would worship the Father in Spirit and in truth.

"When Nicodemus told us of his encounter, I realized that I was not the only one who was confused by his talk of spirit and truth. Such a thought had never been expressed before, at least not to me. I knew I was talking to no ordinary man. Taking a deep breath, I tried to gather a little more courage. All the anger and hostility I had at the beginning of our conversation were quickly melting away. I felt so small and insignificant, and yet...so important and so...so valuable."

Sarah paused to wipe the unbidden tears from her face. "I told him I knew a Messiah would come someday. I didn't dare think what my heart told me was true, but Jesus quieted all my fears. He smiled at me as only Jesus could do and said I was speaking to him."

Sarah's eyes sparkled, and her voice reflected the excitement she had experienced that day. "I was so overjoyed and excited! I had so many questions to ask, and so much to learn. And at the same time, I felt as though my heart was melting into my soul."

She turned to face Peter, who once again had stopped pacing and stood staring at her. Looking straight into his eyes, Sarah said, "I had so many questions to ask, but you and the others came back from town with food. When you looked at me, I could almost read your thoughts." She tried to sound gruff like Peter. "'Who does she think she is? And why is she, a woman of an obviously questionable reputation, defiling our teacher with her presence?'"

Leah giggled, and Sarah smiled as Peter glared at her. "I think you knew better than to say anything." Sarah could not keep the mischievous twinkle from her voice as she added, "I would love to have heard his answer if you had."

Peter glared at her for a moment longer, then muttering to himself, turned to the corner where the darkness would hide his anguished, angry, embarrassed face. In the darkness of that corner, he began again following the steps which had become automatic – forward two steps, turn and repeat his course. His cup turned slowly in his hands with each step that he took.

James still seated near his brother, spoke and everyone turned at the sound of his voice. "I remember that day as if it was yesterday. Your confusion, Sarah, could have been no greater than ours as we approached the well. We didn't want to leave him alone in the first place. It didn't seem safe."

Thomas, who occasionally checked the door, had just opened and closed it softly, hearing nothing unusual. Thomas was generally as cautious as Peter was impetuous. He turned and spoke with his deep bass voice. "That's right. We tried to tell him it wasn't safe for him to stay out there in the middle of nowhere by himself. And beyond that, it made no sense for all of us to go in search of food, leaving him there by the well in the heat with no way to draw water. But, knowing Jesus somewhat by then, we figured he had something in mind."

"When we got back and saw him talking to a Samaritan woman, we were sure the sun had gotten to him," said Nathaniel, chuckling to himself. "I'm sure he knew what we were thinking, just like he did when he saw me under the fig tree before Philip came for me."

"You're right, Sarah," said Andrew. "We would not for the world have questioned his motives or his actions. We simply told him we were back with the food he had sent us to get."

"Do you remember what he said?" asked John, laughing. "You think you were confused, Sarah. After we had walked all that distance in the heat of the day seeking food, he told us he had food that we didn't know about! It was his meat to do the will of God."

Sarah bubbled with laughter. "I saw the look of bewilderment on your faces as I left for the village. I wondered what he had said to you."

Still smiling, Sarah adjusted her hair and straightened her tunic as she continued her story. "I ran to my village to tell everyone about Jesus. I wanted them to feel the joy I felt. They needed to hear Jesus and talk to him themselves. Although I believed he was the Messiah, I was afraid to say for sure he was the Christ, so I just told them what he had told me. Many agreed that he certainly sounded like he was the Christ. Some cynically laughed and said I was crazy. They said I had been in the sun too long. It was all so wonderful that I could almost believe them. Some believed, others went to see Jesus for themselves. When they returned to the village, they, too, were overjoyed, saying I was right. Jesus was the Messiah. They hoped I might be telling the truth and they wanted to believe. After talking to Jesus, they did believe. They had seen and heard for themselves."

A slow smile spread across his face as John added more to the story. "I remember the crowds coming back after you left. From a distance we weren't sure if we were facing an angry mob or just a group of curious people. They came closer to us; we could see that they were excited and hope was written all over their faces."

Andrew smiled, then broke into laughter. "We thought we were confused before, but we really had trouble understanding why Jesus wanted to spend time with Samaritans." Andrew screwed up his face and said the word Samaritans as if he were talking about something unpleasant. This brought laughter from the others because they knew he was not making fun of Sarah, but rather laughing at his own ignorance and former prejudice. "You would think we would have been used to his surprises, but we never ceased to be surprised or confused by him."

Nathaniel joined the mirth. "I know what you mean. When he said we were going to Sychar for a few days, I thought for sure he had been in the sun too long. If I thought nothing good could come out of Nazareth, I was doubly sure nothing worthwhile would be found in Sychar. He proved me wrong again."

"Jesus spent two whole days in our village teaching us about God and life," said Sarah, also laughing with them and feeling much more relaxed now that her story was almost over and they were so accepting of her. "Many lives were changed. My life is different now. I do worship in Spirit and in truth. All the symbols that served as religious reminders are no longer important. The mountain in Samaria will always be a special place for me to worship, but now I worship God wherever I am.

"The Living Water he spoke about wells up within me, bubbling over to anyone who will listen when I speak. I want to tell the world what happened to me. My life now means something. I was telling everyone I met about Jesus, when I heard what was happening here in Jerusalem, I came as quickly as I could."

Sarah was quiet and pensive for a short time. Then with tears again beginning to flow, she said softly, "I would even have gone back to my old way of life to save him from death, but I was too late." Her voice dropped and she was silent for a few seconds that seemed much longer to those who listened intently. They understood.

Sighing deeply, Sarah continued. "When I reached Golgotha, the soldiers were pounding the nails into his hands and then his feet. I watched as they lowered the cross in the foundation hole. His body jerked forward as the cross hit the bottom. It must have hurt terribly, but he had only words of forgiveness for those who hurt him so." Hastily she wiped the streaming tears from her face.

Sarah stood and slowly walked to the table. She filled her cup and paused. With a little more boldness she turned and gazed again into the eyes of Peter. "And now?" she asked. "I don't know for sure why I'm here. My mind says it's over, and yet...my heart says we have not heard the last of our Messiah. I need to stay to do whatever we will be able to do tomorrow – maybe just be there. I need to make it all final, I guess. Then I will return to Sychar and try to convince those who are still weak in faith that there is some kind of logic in it all."

"Logic?" asked Matthew, who had been quietly mulling over the facts in his logical, mathematical mind. "Has there ever been any logic in anything Jesus did? Why did he give Judas the purse strings when I was experienced? Why did he go to Jerusalem when he knew they were waiting for him? And why did he heal the one Peter wounded in the garden? And certainly there is no logic in anyone on a cross wasting precious breath to offer forgiveness to those who put him there! No, there was never any logic in what he did, only love."

Through her tears, Sarah managed the quick smile that was so much a part of her since she met Jesus. "You're right, Matthew. I'm sure he knew a lot more than we could ever begin to understand. There was certainly no logic to him speaking to me – a Samaritan woman. It has taken his death to wake up my mind, but I now know what he meant back there by the well. His words filled my heart with a song." Sarah paused, her eyes closed. Then softly in the minor tones of the Eastern world, with tears flowing, she began singing:

"I came in search of water,
Life's road was hot and dry;
The well so far away and deep,
My parched soul did cry.

'Come drink the Living Water,'
He called to me that day;
The cool refreshing liquid
Washed all my care away.

Then it was I understood
I need not suffer thirst again;
For the well of Living Water
Flows constantly within."

The room was very quiet as the last strains of her song faded. For a brief moment Sarah let the silence hang in the air. Then softly she said, "I cannot bear to give up the faith that he gave me, the belief that my life can be different. I cannot bear to think that I was wrong and he is not the Messiah. I must stay yet awhile. Yes, Peter, I was there. I saw everything. And I felt so helpless."

The Samaritan woman turned away from Peter's intense gaze

and slowly walked back to her corner chair. Her story told, her energy spent, she slowly eased herself onto the chair. Her head dropped wearily into her waiting open hands.

There was a slight rustle of movement and Sarah felt small, comforting arms around her. The child's voice was saying, "It's all right, Sarah. Jesus loves you."

Sarah smiled through her tears, grateful for this uninhibited love of a child. She lifted Leah to her lap, hugging her close. She thought, *No wonder Jesus loved the children.*

Chapter Eight

Sight and Insight

Peter didn't expect the Samaritan woman to be so bold as to speak to them. Nor did he expect the sudden rush of compassion, and even understanding, as he stared at Sarah. Drawn back to the dark void outside the window, he pulled his thoughts and emotions tightly into himself. Combing his fingers through his hair, he wished he could separate his thoughts as easily as his fingers separated his tangled hair. Slow, deliberate movements once again measured his thoughts with each step.

The man who looked like a beggar moved to the table, reached for the goatskin of wine and filled his cup. Peter glanced at the man, wondering who he was. *The face is familiar*, he thought. *I've seen him many times. Why can't I remember his name?* Once again he combed his fingers through his hair and then pulled at a couple of particularly wild strands. *I'm tired of this confusion. I need answers – something to rid my own soul of grief. It really makes no difference who the man is; he's a stranger and shouldn't be here. I've already shared too much of my grief with strangers. I don't need to share any more.*

Following the lead of his random thoughts, Peter once again lashed out. Eyes flashing, finger pointing accusingly at the man, Peter roared like a wounded animal. "Who are you? You couldn't possibly have known Jesus long, so who are you, and why are you here?"

The other disciples were used to Peter's rough ways, but even they flinched. In normal circumstances Peter would not strike out at a stranger like that, and the man was not really a stranger to them.

John started to speak, but changed his mind. The man had a certain confidence about him which, John decided, would speak more clearly than any words he could offer. He waited, believing Joshua could, and would, hold his own with Simon Peter.

Leah whispered to Sarah, "Peter sounds mad, but I bet he's really just not feeling very good because Jesus died and he won't see him anymore."

Sarah hugged her close and whispered back, "You're probably right, Leah."

The little girl shook her head sadly and turned her attention to the man who had received Peter's scathing questions.

Joshua was a small man with graying hair around the temples. His salt and pepper beard seemed to add a maturity to his already forty-some years. Wearing shaggy, gray-brown clothes, he certainly looked more like a beggar than a disciple. The deep lines on his face mirrored a hard life. He was the complete opposite of the stately Nicodemus, who had spoken earlier.

Joshua, keeping his eyes fixed on Peter, took his time in answering. Peter shifted his weight, first to one foot and then the other. Confusion made him unsure of himself. Should he ask his question again, or turn and walk away? Either way, the impetus of the wounded animal roar was lost. Anger drained like sweat from his face, as Joshua continued to stare at him. Finally, Joshua lowered his eyes to his empty cup, as if he would find in it the right words to express his grief. They were not there. He had to search deeper within his soul for them.

Slowly he raised his head, and locking his gray, sparkling eyes with Peter's dark, flashing ones, once again began to speak. "Who am I? You probably remember me as the blind beggar, but my name is Joshua. Those folks are Nathan and Ruth, my parents." He turned and pointed out the elderly couple by a window. They seemed embarrassed by any attention which was given to them.

Joshua looked once more into his empty cup. This time it yielded words to him in a long, steady stream. Turning to Peter, he lifted the cup in front of him, bringing it to eye level so that all could see. "For most of my life I was like this cup, only an empty vessel." He held it briefly there for their attention. He then lowered it and continued to talk.

"I used to sit by the roadside. I think I heard every abusive word that has ever been spoken. Every kick, every jab, and every stone that came my way found its mark and left its scar, but I accepted it all as the way life had to be for me."

Turning the empty cup around and around in his hands, Joshua took a deep breath and continued. "You see, my eyes had been blind since birth, but even the darkness could not hide the hurt and pain I sensed in my parents when people made remarks accusing them of some awful sin. A child born blind was the result of sin. Everyone knew that." There was a slight touch of sarcasm in his voice.

A low groan escaped from Peter's grief-twisted face as recognition slowly sank into the depth of his addled mind. Trying once again to cover his embarrassment, Peter turned to his dark corner to listen to the man's story, which he knew only slightly. John was amazed that Joshua could speak in such a clear matter-of-fact voice with no hint of bitterness.

Ignoring Peter's reaction, Joshua chuckled and glanced at his parents. Then he spoke with some reluctance. "Once I even heard someone say something to my mother which I didn't understand at the time. I was only a small boy, but I will never forget the angry footsteps, followed by a loud crack, as my father moved into action. Even though I could not see, I knew the man would sport a crooked nose the rest of his life."

Joshua again smiled at the elderly couple who sat huddled together. They gasped at their son's words. "I didn't think he knew," whispered Nathan. "He was such a little boy then."

Ruth smiled a sad sort of smile as she remembered the scene. "Neither did I," she whispered back, "but Joshua's right. The man does still have a crooked nose."

"Did your father hit the man in the nose?" asked Leah. This might be her only chance to be included in adult talk. It was a special night and she sensed it would never be repeated.

Joshua couldn't help but feel some empathy for the bewildered parents of the child. There was just too much happening for an inquisitive little girl to keep quiet. And after the strange events of the past few weeks, he wondered if any of the old ways of life would ever return. Somehow he doubted it.

"Yes, little one," said Joshua chuckling. "And don't ask me what he said," he warned, pointing his finger at her, "because some things are not for little girls to hear."

"But you were a little boy when he said it, and you heard," she answered innocently. A little pout was playing around the edges of her mouth.

"Yes, I know, but even I was not supposed to hear. It was an accident." Joshua smiled and she could not stay pouty.

She smiled back at him. "That's okay," she said. "When I get bigger someone will tell me."

It was hard for Leah's parents and brother to hide their amusement at her innocence, but neither did they want to encourage her boldness. Joshua replied wistfully, "Oh, that we could have a world where children didn't have to ever hear such things." All around the room were nods of agreement. Sarah, who was still holding Leah on her lap, hugged her closer as if to protect her.

Joshua paused, reflecting and thinking, then continued. "My parents were good folks who taught me all they could. They loved me beyond words. Instinctively I knew they could not have done any great sin, so I decided, as a very young boy, the fault must be mine. I thought I must be an awfully bad person for God to punish me with blindness. I took the abuse and stood the loneliness as best I could because I believed I deserved it. I tried to contribute to my own living. Every day I sat with my cup begging by the gate of the temple. I hated being helpless. I was becoming bitter with life and with God.

"Then one day, everything changed." Joshua's eyes sparkled as tears threatened to spill over the edge. "Experience taught me the best places to beg, as well as the best time of the day.

"That's where I was that day I heard a large crowd approaching.

Large crowds meant more chance for coins in my cup. Footsteps of all the regular people who passed were familiar sounds to me. Little did I know how much my life would change because of the new sounds I heard. The footsteps stopped by my feet and I braced myself for more abuses, hoping for at least a small coin in exchange.

"One of the strangers spoke. He asked as so many had asked before, 'Teacher,' he said, 'look at this beggar. He's been blind since he was born. Whose fault was it – his or his parents? Who committed the sin?'[1]

"I expected the usual laughter and speculation, but the voice of the one they called Rabbi answered in what will always be musical tones to my ears. 'Neither,' he replied.

"I knew I was blind, but I thought for a minute that my ears also deceived me. It was the first time anyone ever said no one was to blame for my blindness. For the first time in my life someone understood my feelings. It was as if he saw into the very depth of my soul and poured healing oil on a hurt so deep it could not be seen. I knew it was there because I felt the pain. If the rabbi had gone on his way and never said another word without even dropping a coin in my cup, and if I had never met him again, I would still be a different person. All the coins in the world could not have meant as much to me as it did for someone to have a little love and compassion for a blind beggar."

Joshua paused, staring absently into the empty cup in his hands. Peter stood like a marble statue, afraid to take his eyes off Joshua. No one spoke or moved, not wanting to break the spell of his story. Finally, someone scraped a chair across the floor and Joshua blinked, as if he had heard and yet didn't notice the sound.

"I'm not sure what all the rabbi said after that. He talked about revealing the works of God and being the light of the world. I only know I felt warm in my soul. Although I was blind, I thought I might even know what the light was that he talked about. I wanted him to keep talking – about anything – just to hear his voice."

Joshua swept his hand across his eyes. "Then, Jesus touched me." Joshua's voice was husky with emotion. Closing his eyes, he felt the touch of Jesus once more in his soul. "He took me by the hand and lifted me to my feet. I trembled so hard I thought the very pavement shook. I was afraid of what he might do to me. Many times others pretended to have compassion, then beat me, mocked me, and stole what few coins I had in my cup."

Murmurs of disbelief were heard around the room. "That's awful!" "No!" Joshua was surprised. He still was not used to people caring about him or what happened to him. His voice carried a note of awe when he spoke of Jesus.

"His touch was different. It was soft and gentle, and yet firm and commanding. It was almost like the loving way my mother used to hold me when other children laughed at me and hit me. My fear soon turned to excitement – even expectation. I knew deep within my soul that something extraordinarily wonderful was about to happen. But never in my wildest dreams would I have guessed the miracle about to be mine."

Again Joshua's hand went to his eyes. "Jesus smoothed something over my closed eyelids. I recognized its smell; and as it began to harden, I knew it was clay. I used to make toys with it when I was little. Then, the rabbi told me to go wash in the pool of Siloam."

"I like to play with clay," said Leah. "I make furniture for my dolls. Did you go right away? How did you find the pool if you couldn't see? Was the water...?"

"Leah!" Adam gave her a silencing stare. "Let the man talk. I'm sure he'll tell us everything, if a certain little girl will stop asking so many questions."

"I just wanted to know," said Leah with her lower lip quivering into a pout.

"That's all right, Leah," said Sarah, hugging the child close to her. "I'm sure Joshua will answer your questions in time."

"All right," said Leah and settled back against Sarah to listen to Joshua.

Joshua smiled at Leah. His voice still vibrated with excitement as he remembered that day. "Believe me, I didn't wait to be told a second time to go to Siloam. The rabbi's voice, though it was kind and compassionate, had a note of authority which I knew I must obey. As quickly as my legs would carry a body that could not see where it was going, I made my way to the pool. I heard splashing and people talking, so I knew I was near. Someone took my arm and asked if I needed help. Gratefully, I accepted his guidance. I hadn't thought about how I would get to the water without falling into the pool. The man led me to the edge. When I told him I needed to wash my eyes, he cupped his hands and held the water for me. He didn't ask why, and I couldn't have told him if he had.

"As the cool waters of Siloam washed away the clay, I began to feel a pain in my eyes. At first it didn't make sense to me, then I realized it must be light! For the first time in my life the darkness became piercing light. I could see!"

The excitement in Joshua's voice was contagious. All around the room, friends listened with hopeful anticipation. "The man who had helped me became a blurry figure in front of me," Joshua continued. "I got so excited I almost knocked him into the pool."

Leah giggled. In her imagination she could see the man flailing his arms, trying to get out of the pool.

Joshua laughed, too. "It was great! The man took my trembling arms in his and looked into my eyes. I saw him looking at me! Do you know I never saw eyes before? Or a face? Or a person for that matter! Words can never explain all the emotions that ran through me."

"Did he get mad because you almost knocked him in the water?" asked Leah.

"Oh no, not at all," answered Joshua. "He smiled tentatively. He had no idea what was going on. But for me, it was beautiful to see a mouth – to see what a smile looked like. When I told him what had happened, that smile covered his whole face, all the way to his eyes. It was just too wonderful for words. We danced around the pool like a couple of mad men. I was laughing and babbling like one too. 'My parents,' I said. 'I've got to find my parents!' I was so excited that I didn't know what to say or do. The man understood. As I hurried away, he wished me God speed. I didn't even have sense enough to get his name. I hope someday I will meet him again and be able to thank him."

"I bet that people laughed at you for acting like that," said Leah, still giggling. Everyone was laughing so hard it brought tears to the eyes. The difference between tears of joy and tears of sorrow can not always be distinguished.

"Yes," said Joshua, dabbing at his own wet eyes. "They sure did. Most were glad for me, but some were jealous. No one understood. I didn't either, but I didn't care. I just wanted to find my parents and see what they looked like. I ran through the streets in search of my house and parents. I still experienced some pain in my eyes. So many questions arose I wondered if I would ever find the answers. I wondered if everyone has pain with sight. Then I wondered if I would feel pain when I could see others who suffered as I had. And did the man who healed me feel my pain because he could see it in me? I hoped it would soon go away. I could see for the first time in my life and I wanted to enjoy it."

"Gee," said Leah. "You ask as many questions as I do. Did you get any answers to yours?"

Joshua smiled at the little girl. "Well, yes, I did, at least to some of them. I think Jesus felt my pain. And I think if we really see our brothers and sisters suffering, we will feel their pain – and joy. The man at the pool felt both with me."

"I think so, too." Leah tried very hard to sound grown-up.

Joshua continued, pausing to wipe away fresh tears. He felt a little foolish, but simply could not keep the tears of joy back. "It was strange trying to find my way home. I even had to close my eyes several times to get my bearings. There was so much to see I wanted to stop and look at everything, but I had to find my home and share the news with those two wonderful folks who stood by me all my life.

"Finally, I came to the place where I was begging and I knew I was not far from home. People stopped me and asked questions. People I had known for years only as voices and footsteps suddenly became images. We were all confused. They couldn't believe I was the one who begged for a living. Some said I must be someone who just looked like the beggar. I could understand that. Everyone I saw looked so different from the picture I had in my mind of them. I found it hard to believe my own eyes."

"You mean you never saw the kids you played with?" asked Leah.

"I never had many friends," said Joshua. "The other kids weren't allowed to play with me because I was blind. Their parents assumed a great sin caused it, and therefore I was not fit to play with their children."

"Were they afraid of you?" asked Leah, surprised that anyone would have no friends at all.

Joshua's brow knit in thought. "Afraid? Possibly. People are often afraid of what they don't understand."

"I bet they were excited when they learned you could see."

"Not so much excited as curious," he replied. "No one ever heard of such a thing before. Some people took a 'watch and wait' attitude. Others, since they could not understand what had happened, drew back in fear. Some tried to touch me, hoping my healing would rub off on them."

Joshua chuckled. "It was almost funny that they were afraid of me, the blind beggar they abused for so many years."

Nathaniel stopped at the table as he wandered around the room. "Maybe they had reason to be afraid," he said.

"I suppose they did," replied Joshua. "They probably thought I would remember and try to get even. Since the people didn't understand what was happening, they decided to take me to the Pharisees, certain they would be able to explain. It was their job to interpret such miracles. Personally, I didn't care much about an explanation. I knew I was healed, and not just of my blindness. All the old anger and hurt over who was responsible was gone. When Jesus gave me sight in my eyes, he gave me insight into my soul as well. I didn't really want to see the Pharisees. I just wanted to see my parents, but the crowd pressed around me until I didn't have much choice. I was swept along like a leaf on a fast-moving stream."

"What did the Pharisees do? Were they kind to you? Did they

know who Jesus was? What..."

"Leah!" her brother interrupted.

"I just wanted to know," she said peevishly.

"Well, give the man a chance. I'm sure he'll tell you what you want to know if you stop interrupting with so many questions," said Adam.

Joshua smiled at her and winked. She smiled back and he continued with the story.

"They asked me over and over and over again to tell them what happened. I told them as clearly as I knew how the rabbi had made some kind of ointment from the clay, put it on my eyes, and told me to go wash in Siloam. I followed his directions and now I could see. What more could I say? But they weren't satisfied.

"It was hard to concentrate when they kept repeating the same questions. I was fascinated by all the colors, the textures, and the people, all the things I could see for the first time in my life. And the decorations of the Temple! They almost took my breath away. I never imagined such beauty! I tried to pay attention. I even closed my eyes so I could concentrate, but one of the Pharisees yelled at me to look at him when he was talking.

"They were upset because it was the Sabbath!" Joshua tried to make his face look pious and his voice sound like the righteous Pharisees. "Some said, 'the man can't be from God. He did this...this act on the Sabbath and everyone knows God doesn't work on the Sabbath! The man has to be a sinner.'"

Leah giggled. The others also smiled and chuckled at his imitations of the Pharisees. Nicodemus laughed heartily. "That sounds like some folks we know and work with," he said. "Right, Joseph?"

Joseph, also laughing, nodded in agreement. "I could almost name him, but I won't."

Joshua grinned self-consciously and continued, trying to sound like the confused Pharisees and concerned neighbors. "Others asked, 'Has anyone ever heard of a sinner giving sight to the blind?'"

Joshua paused, shaking his head. Then he proceeded. "They argued among themselves until I felt my head spinning."

"Why didn't they just find Jesus and ask him to explain what he did?" asked Leah.

"They didn't know where he was, or who he was," answered Joshua. "I thought they would want to find Jesus first and learn the truth from him instead of wasting time with a poor beggar. They were more concerned with the breaking of the rules of the Sabbath. They asked me again what had happened and what I thought about the man."

"Didn't they hear you the first time?" asked Leah.

"Oh, they heard me all right," answered Joshua, shifting his position and turning the empty cup in his hand. He still wasn't used to seeing people stare at him – even when they were compassionate and caring.

"I was really amazed. Here they were, learned, distinguished leaders of the synagogue, and they were asking me, an unlearned, formerly blind beggar, what I thought! I tried to keep a straight face as I did the best I could. I repeated what I had already told them and said I thought he was probably a prophet. I don't know why I bothered. For that matter, I don't know why they bothered to ask me. They didn't really listen to me, and they certainly didn't believe me. Instead they decided to send for my parents and ask them to explain.

"I was beginning to be annoyed with them – Pharisees or not. I just wanted to get out of there and find my parents. I didn't know that some of our neighbors saw me and ran to get them. There was a commotion outside and one of the Pharisees said, 'Bring the man's parents in here. We'll prove this man's a liar.' I held my breath as they were led into the room. I wondered if they would know me, or if they would admit it if they did. Until I heard their voices, I couldn't even be sure they were my parents."

Joshua glanced toward his parents, love and compassion for them filling his eyes. They nodded. "That's right," said Ruth in a small voice. She wasn't used to speaking in a group of any kind. "I was scared to death, sure it was some kind of trick. When they asked me how our son could see, I had no idea what they were talking about. My son, born blind, was blind when he left that morning. I didn't expect to see him until evening."

The plump little lady's face beamed with joy through her tears. Ruth felt incredible awe for her son's healing. She wiped her eyes and her husband continued. "They asked us if that man was our son. I guess they weren't so much interested in proving he had been healed as they were in proving he was not the same one who had been blind and begged for a living."

Nathan looked at his son with reverence. He worked hard to take care of his wife and son who had been blind. He took abuse, as did his wife, but they loved their son. The wrinkled face told the story of Nathan's three score and ten years. His hands shook a little as he reached toward his wife with a gesture of protection and love.

Ruth continued, "It was an easy question to answer. Of course he was our son."

With hardly a pause in rhythm, Nathan picked up her words Almost fifty years of synchronized living together created a husband and wife team who simply thought as two who had become one. "We couldn't tell them how he had gained his sight. We weren't there when it happened. So we simply told them they should ask him. He was an adult and could speak for himself. Just because he was blind did not mean he was also deaf and dumb."

The attention was returned to Joshua. Eagerly they all waited for him to continue his story. "Did they believe you then?" Leah wasn't too shy to ask the questions they all were thinking.

"Not yet. I was so afraid when they had my parents brought in, not sure what they would to do to them. What a way to see your parents for the first time in your life! My heart swelled with praise for God. I wanted to heap hugs and kisses on these two, who were at last more than just voices to me, but my feet felt as if they were firmly planted to the floor. I could only stand and stare."

Joshua smiled broadly and then chuckled a little. "I was proud of the way they boldly answered the Pharisees. I let out the breath I had been holding when I realized they did recognize me! I was different and could no longer contribute to their income by begging, but they still had confidence in me. I was proud to be their son."

Joshua swiped his sleeve across his eyes and swallowed a gulp of air. Squaring his shoulders and lifting his chin slightly, he continued his story. "The Pharisees weren't very happy. They turned to me and shouted, 'Give God the glory. We know the man you speak of is a sinner.' Can you imagine? They thought Jesus was a sinner because he healed me on the Sabbath. Of course I didn't know yet who Jesus was, so I told them I didn't know if he was a sinner or not. I didn't know anything about him. I only knew the bare facts, which were: I had been born blind and now I could see. It was evident to me that a miracle had taken place. They asked me one more time what he had done to me and how he had opened my eyes.

"I was getting more than a little weary of the game-playing. It was not the truth they wanted to hear, but their preconceived notion of what truth was. They only wanted me to tell them what they wanted to hear. The room became so quiet you could almost hear the sound of sheep on the hillside outside the city. I glanced around the room. No one seemed to be breathing. It was almost as if they had all turned to stone and I, alone, had breath in me. I thought, maybe they want to find this man who made me see because a miracle has occurred.

"Finally, I asked, 'Why do you keep asking me over and over what happened? Do you want to become his disciples? Do you want to invite him to work more signs and miracles? Do you also want to believe?'"

Joshua paused, lost in his thoughts for a few seconds. Then he smiled. "Those stone figures suddenly came to life. "It wasn't very likely they wanted Jesus for any good reason. I wasn't even sure they were capable of recognizing a miracle. For Pharisees they certainly were dense. Of course, I didn't say what I really thought." Joshua smiled and winked at Leah, who giggled.

Nicodemus laughed. "I wish I had been there that day. I heard about it, of course, but I missed it."

"We didn't hear it quite that way Joshua tells it, however," Joseph added with a broad grin.

Joshua smiled at them and resumed his story. "The anger of the Pharisees that day almost matched the violence of that storm we had

Friday. I didn't know it was humanly possible for so much anger to be within one person, but one of the Pharisees became so red in the face I was afraid he would explode right then and there. I began backing away, not wanting to be in his path if he should. Others eased back, getting ready to run. The Pharisee took one step toward me, punching at me with his fat little finger to emphasize his words. That pompous little Pharisee shouted, 'You are his disciple.'

"He took one step forward and I took one back. He jabbed at me again. 'We follow Moses,' he yelled.

"We took another step.

"'We know that God spoke to Moses,' he shouted.

"One more step backward.

"'As for this man you speak about, we don't even know where he came from.'

"Finally, I was backed against a pillar. By this time I could contain myself no longer. Astonishment at their ignorance freed me from fear. I, who had not even seen a tree or a bird or a flower, much less my own parents, could now see more clearly than they, who'd had sight in their eyes from birth. It was incredible! So I guess I got a little carried away."

"Just a little," remarked his father dryly.

Joshua grinned and ignored the remark. "Feeling an unaccustomed boldness, with my hands on my hips, I began pushing forward. The man had to back up or be stepped on. 'Why, this is marvelous!' I said. I didn't jab at him the way he had jabbed me, but I felt like it. 'You don't know where he came from and yet he gave me sight! Have you ever been able to open the eyes of the blind? You say that God doesn't listen to sinners – that God only hears people who worship him. Have you ever heard of anyone else who has done what that man did? With all your power, wisdom, and knowledge, is it possible for you to do these things? Personally I say if the man weren't from God, he could have done nothing. As far as I know, only God can give that kind of power.'"

"Wow! I bet they were really mad at you then," said Leah.

"Oh yes, they were extremely angry by then. The haughty little man turned ashen. I was afraid he might fall dead on the spot. This time he didn't push. He held his hands at his sides with his fists clenched so tightly his knuckles turned white.

"He yelled, 'Who do you think you are that you can teach us – you who were born in sin? Get out!' He swung his arm around and pointed to the way out. 'Don't ever come back in this synagogue again. Go find your rabbi and follow him.'

"That left me a bit shaken. Because of all that had happened that day, the miracle followed by such anger and fear, I wasn't sure which way to turn. As a blind beggar, I had never been allowed to worship in the Temple anyway. Would I never be allowed to praise God for the miracle of healing he had given to me? I was sure God must have heard my prayers even though they were not official, but what if they were right? Now that I had sight and was no longer a beggar, would God still care about me? What if God would only listen to me if I came to the Temple at the proper times?

"People started scattering, afraid to speak to me for fear of what the Pharisees might do or say to them. They couldn't have scattered more quickly if someone had yelled 'Fire!' I wondered if my parents would leave me also. I didn't have to worry long. They approached me with tears in their eyes and we left together."

"I would find them and kick them in the shins!" Leah had her fists ready. Sarah held her close to keep her from jumping up and running out in search of the bad guys.

Joshua set his cup on the table and moved to her side. Taking her small fists and cupping them in his big hands, he gently opened her fingers. He said lovingly, "I don't think Jesus would want that. God will judge them."

Leah looked belligerent and then contrite. Tears ran down her cheeks. "I know, but I miss Jesus and they shouldn't have been so mean to you and to him."

"You're right, Leah, but Jesus gave me sight. I can tolerate the rest. And he gave you a special blessing of a beautiful family, as well as a strong spirit."

Sarah held her close and Joshua went back to his story.

111

"Once I was outside, I tried to get my bearings. My parents were pointing me in the direction of home when a man approached me. The footsteps were familiar, but I waited to hear his voice. I looked at my parents for help. They had no idea who he was.

"Then he asked, 'Joshua, do you believe in the Son of God?'

"I knew he was talking about the one who had healed me, so I asked, 'Who is he, and where is he? I want to believe!'"

"Didn't you know who Jesus was yet?" asked Leah.

"Well, it's true he healed me, but I was blind until I washed in Siloam. Jesus wasn't at the pool when my sight came to me, so I never saw him. However, I sensed who he was, and I could never forget that voice. I guess I just wanted to hear it from his own lips. I wanted to be certain. He smiled at me and spoke as if he had read my thoughts. 'Yes, Joshua, I am he.' Again I felt such a flood of joy and peace that I could only fall on my knees at his feet."

John was there that day and remembered the red, angry faces of the Pharisees who had followed Joshua out of the Temple. "You're right, Joshua." John took a sip from his cup and faced Joshua. "I remember the look on the faces of those frustrated men as they stood on the Temple steps, shaking their fists and shouting unintelligible words at you. Jesus said blindness is not always in the eyes. We all knew he was right. In your own days of darkness you knew and understood far more about the pain, loneliness and anguish of people."

Joshua smiled. "Blindness is a difficult way of life, but the darkness I lived with was nothing in comparison to the oppressing lack of light that covered the earth when Jesus hung on that cross."

John slowly turned his cup in his hand. "It was about the darkest that I have ever seen – even more so than the many times we have been caught out in the sea by a sudden storm. It was almost like the inner evil of all humankind must have joined forces that day." John shook his head, still having a hard time believing it.

"That's true," said Joshua. "But remember, Jesus told us he was the Light. As surely as the sun drove away that awful darkness while he hung there lifeless on the cross, the Son of God will drive away the darkness of the human soul."

Joshua paused picked up his still-empty cup and stood for a moment or two gazing into it. Lifting his eyes to meet Peter's steady stare, he answered his earlier question, "Yes, Peter, I was at Golgotha. I saw Jesus' pain and remembered my own. I remembered the times I had been kicked, stoned, and spat upon. Derisive words of people accusing me or my parents of sin still rang in my ears. His words healed my pain when he said I was not to blame for my blindness. When he said to the thief on the cross beside him, 'You will be with me,' once again I heard his words to me, 'I am he.' I am here tonight because Jesus gave me new life – the new birth about which Nicodemus spoke. He gave me sight for these once-blind eyes and insight for my blinded spirit. I will stay surrounded by the comfort of kindred spirits until morning, when we can go to the tomb. After that? God willing I will travel throughout Galilee and tell my story to anyone who will listen."

Joshua reached for the goat skin, his eyes still locked with Peter's eyes. Finally dropping his gaze, Joshua filled his cup and started to turn away. He paused and turned back to face Peter. "You see, Peter, my life was an empty vessel waiting to be filled. Now it is as full as this cup. My life is full of the Living Water." This he said as he turned to Sarah. He raised his cup in salute to her and smiled. Then he returned to his place beside his parents.

Peter stared for a minute, opened his mouth to say something, but closed it without uttering a sound. Again his slow, deliberate, measured two-step pace engulfed his weary body and spirit.

Chapter Nine

Called From Death

Joshua's eyes, which formerly held no sight, sparkled from the miracle he received. He took his freshly-filled cup and returned to his parents' side. Beside them Nicodemus, Joseph and the Samaritan woman slipped into their own thoughts. Leah began to doze again on Sarah's lap. Candles were losing their height. Weariness settled on all of them.

Peter nervously stepped off his anxiety in his self-chosen space by the window, stopping occasionally to pound a fist furtively into the palm of his hand and mutter, "Why?"..."Now what do we do?"..."Why didn't he listen?"

Sensing someone behind him, Peter turned so abruptly that he nearly collided with Lazarus, who stood facing him with an indulgent smile on his face. He placed a hand on Peter's shoulder. Peter, about to pull away and snap at him, thought better of it. He was so absorbed with his own thoughts, and in the dim light of the room, he momentarily didn't recognize Lazarus. Focusing on the indulgent smile, Peter tried to conceal his own puzzled frown.

Sighing deeply, he turned back to Lazarus, started to speak, coughed, cleared his throat and tried again, giving voice to his thoughts. "How can you smile, Lazarus?" he asked. There was no hint of anger – only confusion and sadness. "I'm sure you were there. You saw what they did to him." Peter, looking into the eyes of his friend, slowly asked a question they all had been pondering. "Is it possible that you know something the rest of us don't know?"

Peter's voice was beginning to lose some of the earlier harshness and bitterness. Even a hint of hope could be detected once in a while – especially when he let the calming influence of Lazarus soothe his frazzled nerves. Hearing the stories of others had begun to strengthen his faltering hope. *Maybe it's possible Jesus understands my denial as well as he understood these others who have shared their stories. Could Jesus really forgive me?*

"Sit down, my friend, and relax a little. You're making us all tired with your constant movement. It won't bring the dawn any sooner, you know." Lazarus continued to smile.

Peter stared at him for as long as he could, then smiled weakly, shrugged his shoulders, and found an empty chair close to the window where Mary sat. Wearily he dropped onto it. Unable to sit still, however, he found a loose thread on his tunic and began to pick at it.

"Yes, Peter," answered Lazarus. "You know I was there. You know my story well, at least most of it. It's so incredible that I, too, feel I must share my experience with you. There are some things which I have never shared with anyone – not even my sisters. I believe now is the time."

Lazarus, brother of Mary and Martha of Bethany, and long-time friend of Jesus, looked radiant, even though he had been through some trying times. He was not a big man. Neither was he necessarily muscular, yet he gave the impression that he could hold his own in any kind of trouble. Although only in his mid-thirties, Lazarus seemed to possess the wisdom of one much older. Content with life itself, he enabled others to feel at ease.

Everyone in the room knew Lazarus was raised from the dead. Those who saw the man emerge from four days in the tomb would never forget! Lazarus had been reluctant to talk about it. Now, listening intently, each one waited to hear his story from the beginning. Even Leah, waking as Lazarus spoke, sat quietly on Sarah's lap.

He pulled a chair nearer the candlelight where he could see and be seen, not that he wanted the attention. He just wanted everyone to feel comfortable. Lazarus began his story with the soothing tones of one with self-assurance. "My friendship with Jesus goes way back.

We first met many years ago as children when our families went to Jerusalem for the festivals. The road through Bethany is one of the main routes to Jerusalem, so a lot of people stream through our little town each year.

"One year when we were about twelve or thirteen, Mary and Joseph came from Nazareth a few days early. We had a lot of time before the Passover festival just to have fun and enjoy each other's company. We played games with the other boys in the neighborhood. When we lost in games, we still felt good about the way we had played. Even then Jesus' passion for truth and honesty had its effect on all who knew him.

"We both loved reading the Torah, so we talked about our lessons a lot of the time. He seemed to grasp their meaning more quickly than I and would explain things to me in ways I could understand.

"After the festival that year, my parents, sisters and I returned to our home in Bethany. Mary and Joseph stayed over in Jerusalem so they could get an early start for Galilee the next morning. They could not stay with us on the return trip because they were traveling back with a caravan which was routed a different way. Almost two days later, we were awakened just before daybreak by a knock at the door. My father rushed to the door to find Mary and Joseph standing there. Mary was tearful – almost hysterical." Lazarus smiled as he glanced toward Mary. She returned his smile, knowing well the story he was about to tell.

"They asked us if Jesus was at our home. They had thought he was among friends or relatives, but when they made camp for the night, after a thorough search of the camp, they realized he wasn't with the caravan at all.[1] That was bad enough, but they weren't even sure if he started out with them. Maybe he missed the caravan completely and was lost and alone in Jerusalem.

"Filled with panic, they began immediately back-tracking along a dangerous path. When they couldn't find him among their relatives, they thought possibly he went home with us, or at least I might know where he was."

"Was he really lost?" asked Leah.

"Well," said Lazarus, smiling, "Jesus knew where he was, but his parents didn't. So I guess you could say he was lost from them. But Jesus always knew where he was and where he was going. I couldn't imagine him knowingly hurting anyone.

"I knew how much he loved the Temple and the reading of the scrolls. So, as I pulled on my tunic, I suggested he might be in the Temple. It was early morning and my parents and Mary and Joseph couldn't imagine him in the Temple at that time of day. Surely someone would have sent him home. I knew how easily Jesus could lose track of time when he was reading and discussing the Torah with the rabbis. There was a shortcut I often used, so I offered to go with them.

"Taking them across the valley path, we returned to the Temple in Jerusalem just as the sun popped over the horizon. Sure enough, he was there. Not only was Jesus listening to the teachers, but he was discussing the words of Moses with such wisdom and intelligence that the teachers were amazed. Suddenly Mary's fear and anxiety turned to a funny combination of anger and relief. I turned to say something to her and saw her expression change. I thought, Oh boy! He's in for it now!"

Lazarus paused, chuckling to himself. Mary also smiled. He continued. "She scolded Jesus and took him by the hand the way she used to do when he was younger. He was astonished. I don't think he even realized how long he'd been there. I heard him say, 'But, Mother, surely you knew where I would be! I had to learn my Father's business!'"

Lazarus smiled again. He glanced at Mary, who was smiling through the tears. She spoke softly, but her voice was clear. "I was so scared when I realized he wasn't with the caravan. I was angry with myself for not checking on him soon after we left Jerusalem. I thought he was old enough to give him some freedom, but I didn't expect that much freedom!

"All the way back to Bethany, Joseph and I kept telling each other he would be at the home of Lazarus. We really believed he would be there by the time we arrived at the home of our friends. I didn't even realize how early in the morning it was until their father came to the door. I could tell we got him out of bed. I felt awful, but I was so anxious I couldn't wait until later.

"I was glad Lazarus knew a shortcut. I couldn't rest until Jesus was found. When we went inside the temple and found Jesus talking to the rabbis as if nothing else in the world mattered, I was overwhelmingly relieved, but the pent-up anxiety exploded into anger. I would have scolded him more if Joseph hadn't stopped me. Dear Joseph. He always seemed to know the right thing to do."

Lazarus laughed. "It wasn't funny for you at the time, I know, but I could not keep from laughing at the amazed look on his face and the changing expression on yours. I'm glad my mother didn't go along with us. She would have scolded me good for laughing.

"His words were strange, though – about learning his Father's business, that is. I was glad you came home with me and spent the rest of that day and night in our home. You and Joseph were exhausted and simply could not have begun the long trip back to Galilee.

"Jesus and I took our mats up to the roof. It was warm and comfortable – a good night for sleeping, but we didn't sleep much. We talked most of the night. I asked him what he meant back in the Temple about learning his Father's business. Joseph was a carpenter. How could he learn to be a carpenter in the Temple? And besides that, Joseph had already begun to teach him the trade."

Lazarus leaned back in his chair, pulling the memories from the depth of his mind. "Jesus sat there on his mat so quietly that I thought for a minute he had fallen asleep. He was gazing into the sky, lost in concentration. I thought, *he's counting the stars, or maybe he doesn't hear me.* I started to repeat my question. Putting his finger to his mouth, he silenced me. He seemed to be listening to something or someone. I watched him. He had such a look of serenity. Then he nodded, as if acknowledging a statement or question, turned to me, and said he was talking with his Father. He was ready to share his identity with me, but I would have to promise to keep his secret until the time was right.

"I asked him how I would know when the time was right. He

said, 'You'll know.' We were always so close. He knew his secret would be safe with me, but I gave him my word anyway. I listened as Jesus told me Joseph wasn't his real father. God was. He was sent to bring salvation and someday, when the time was fulfilled, he would leave Nazareth and train disciples.

"What he told me would have been unbelievable from anyone else. It was more than just the dream of a young man's future. Even then, a note of authority and determination was in his voice. I didn't understand all of what he said – or even very much of it – but when he was finished, I believed him and I honored my word. I told no one, not even my sisters. He said when the time was right I would have a story to tell. I think the time is right."

Lazarus paused, reflecting and organizing his thoughts. *Where do I begin?* He took the cup Martha offered, smiled at her, and took a sip. "We spent days together, either in his home or mine, as often as we could. I don't think anyone ever enjoyed life any more than he did. He found a story or something exciting in anything and everything in creation – whether the lilies growing in the field or the sparrow building its nest."

"Jesus is the best storyteller in the world," Leah interrupted.

"Was," corrected her brother.

"Oh," she said, quietly. "I forgot."

"Let Lazarus continue his story," replied her brother, not unkindly.

"I'm sorry I interrupted," said Leah. "What happened then?"

Adam was surprised by his sister's apology. *Maybe there's hope for this child yet*, he thought.

Lazarus smiled at them. Adam reminded him of himself when he was younger. "I talked my sisters into going along with me to watch the baptism at the river. We heard John preaching in that booming voice as we approached." Lazarus tried to make his voice sound booming like John's. "'Repent! Be baptized. I'm not important. Someone else is coming who is so great I am not even worthy to untie his sandals and bathe his feet. I am only preparing his way.'"[2]

Martha looked at him and said with a note of loving sarcasm, "You don't really sound like John the Baptist, you know. Maybe you need the scratchy wool coat and some locusts and honey. That would be enough to make anyone shout."

Lazarus, surprised at Martha's unexpected wit, laughed heartily with the others. "You're right, Martha. I admit I'm not much of an imitator, especially of John. No one could imitate him. He was surely unique. But he had a message to tell – one that a lot of folks missed.

"I knew he was talking about Jesus and wondered if the time was right. I dared not say anything because I promised Jesus I wouldn't. While we listened and watched, we saw Jesus approaching. He waved. We waved back. John saw him, too, and shouted, 'Look! Here he comes now. There's the one I told you about.'

"My sisters looked puzzled and Mary started to say something. I knew she would ask me if I knew what John meant. I couldn't lie to her and I couldn't ignore her or tell her what I knew. So I tried a little diversion."

Mary gave her brother a puzzled look and then she laughed. "I wondered about your foolish gibberish. I didn't see any connection between what John said and your comment about the birds."

Lazarus chuckled. "I know. I said something really stupid like, 'See those sparrows over there? I wonder if they have a nest around here.' It was enough. Mary just shook her head and turned back to watch the baptism.

"It really surprised me when Jesus went into the Jordan for baptism. I was even more surprised by the events which followed. We've already heard about the dove and the loud, thunderous voice. Suddenly, I began to understand our talks from childhood. Somehow I knew it was not yet time, so I continued to honor our friendship and keep our secret."

Leah looked puzzled. "It must have been awfully hard not to say anything when you knew so much. I have a hard time keeping a secret."

"You have a hard time keeping quiet," said her brother with a mixture of sarcasm and love.

Lazarus laughed. "It was hard sometimes. But I promised him I wouldn't tell, so I had to keep my promise."

Lazarus drained his cup and set it on the table. Then thoughtfully he continued. "As was said earlier, Jesus started toward the wilderness. I ran to catch up with him. Knowing he would need time to think and plan, I just walked with him for a little while in silence. Then I offered to go with him.

"At the edge of the wilderness we stopped. He laid his hand on my arm and thanked me for my offer, but it was something he had to do alone. He told me our friendship would help him face questions he knew he had to answer. As we've already heard, he had some tough struggles and decisions which he alone could answer. He told me to take care of my sisters and said he would see me later. He went to the wilderness, and Mary, Martha and I returned to Bethany."

Lazarus glanced at Peter, who was still seated, unconsciously picking at the threads of his tunic. He smiled to himself and continued. "When Jesus began his ministry, I joined him as often as I could. He started choosing men as his disciples. We were so close I assumed I would be chosen, so I felt more than a little hurt when he didn't ask me. One day I gathered enough courage to ask him why.

"He told me I was already his very close friend whom he loved – closer even than his own brothers at times. He said I understood him better than anyone and knew more about him than anyone else ever would. Even if I didn't understand, he knew I would stand by him. But he said I was needed where I was, and when the time was right, I would be very important to his ministry. I didn't understand, but I didn't seek further. He had his reasons. I could be content to stay in Bethany and more or less look after Mary and Martha, especially after our parents died."

"Did he say he looked after us?" asked Martha, pausing in her busyness to look at Mary.

Mary smiled and winked at Lazarus. "I can't be certain, Martha, but I thought we looked after him – or to be more correct, you took care of all of us."

"Humph!" sniffed Martha as she continued her course around the room, making sure everyone was comfortable, filling cups and straightening things that didn't really need to be straightened. "How soon we forget!" she said with a twinkle in her eye and a note of mischief in her voice. She was grateful to have Lazarus teasing her as he had always done.

"Well, all right," he grinned at them. "I must say, Martha managed quite well. She really didn't need my help, or interference as she called it."

Lazarus paused and glanced at his sisters thoughtfully with a hint of mischief in his eyes. "Do you remember that one time when Jesus came for a visit?"[3]

Martha frowned, pretending ignorance. "Jesus came to our house many times."

Lazarus responded, "I know. But I'm talking about the time a few months back when Jesus came and brought all of the disciples with him."

Mary snickered. "I remember. Martha cleaned house and cooked for days. And still things weren't quite the way she wanted them."

"Oh, yes," replied Martha blushing. "I remember." She was glad the room was dimly lit to help hide her chagrin.

"Martha could really stir up a hornet's nest when she got busy," said Lazarus, still grinning at his sisters. "Like Mary said, she cleaned the house for days. Mary and I had our hiding places." He winked at Mary.

Martha scowled at him, but had to eventually smile. Martha loved her brother and was used to his teasing. She knew he would tell the story no matter how hard she tried to divert his attention.

"When Jesus finally arrived," Lazarus continued, "poor Martha was beside herself with worry and fatigue. But I couldn't believe my ears when she actually complained to Jesus, asking him to make Mary help her. If I answered her the way Jesus did, I would've been wearing a pot around my neck. He told her to sit down and stop stewing – well, maybe not in those exact words, but close. Martha just stared at him. I could almost hear her thinking, I don't believe you said that!"

Martha's voice was weak and halting, almost a whisper, "You're right, Lazarus. I did wonder how he could say such a thing to me after I worked so hard. And then I realized what a fool I was. I wanted to run, but Jesus took my hand and said 'Martha, Martha. Don't be anxious. Come join us. We're all friends.'"

Lazarus went to his sister and put his arm around her shoulder. "Jesus appreciated all the work you did. However, he was more interested in you."

"I know." She smiled in spite of her tears. "Having things clean and nice and setting a good table were important to me. It was always easy for you and Mary to sit and listen to the birds sing, watch the colors of the sunset, and especially listen to Jesus talk when he came to visit. I wanted to listen, but believed someone had to take care of details. I often resented having to work so hard while Mary could relax and enjoy life. Jesus made me realize work was my choice. No one forced me to do it. Mary chose to sit and learn. I needed to examine my choices – at least be aware they were mine to make."

Lazarus smiled and returned to the table to fill his cup. He stood staring into the light of the candle so long some thought he would never finish his story. No one made a sound – not even Leah.

Finally, still standing by the table, he spoke again, softly, "We tried to keep up with all his travels. We jotted down bits and parts of every story we heard so we could ask him about them the next time he stopped on his way either to or from Jerusalem. We were concerned about the rumors that reached us.

"We heard he had angered the authorities in Jerusalem. Jesus tried to tell them who he was, but they wouldn't listen to him or believe him. Instead, they tried to stone him. I planned to go to him, and then I became very ill.[4] I don't know what hit me, but I got very weak, couldn't eat or drink. Never had I experienced such pain before. My sisters wanted to send for Jesus. I wouldn't let them. They argued that he had healed many people with so many different illnesses, surely he could heal his friend. We heard that he had just recently given sight to a man who had been born blind." Lazarus turned to Joshua and smiled. "It is good to meet that person and know the difference it made in his life."

Lazarus paused, then continued. "I wouldn't let them take

advantage of our friendship. I knew his life would be in danger if he appeared anywhere near Jerusalem. I was sure I would get better soon. After all, Jesus promised me someday I would be important to his ministry in a way none other could be. He healed many people. One more certainly would not be unique. So, I thought, I had to get well to do whatever he had in mind for me to do. Unfortunately I didn't get better. I was so sick I thought I would die. As a matter of fact, I guess I did – die, that is!"

Even though everyone in the room knew about his experience, it was still disturbing to hear it spoken – and from his own lips. The room became quiet as each one tried to imagine how Lazarus could be in the room with them when he had been dead. A sudden flickering of a candle startled them, as if a cord by which they hung onto his every word had been severed, dropping them with a sudden crash into the present moment.

Lazarus shifted in his seat and resumed his story while someone lit another candle and set in place. "My sisters tell me I slept in an unconscious sleep for several days. They were so frightened they sent for Jesus anyway, but he didn't come immediately." Lazarus smiled softly. "Poor Martha was really beside herself that time. She was so sure if only Jesus would come everything would be all right again."

Lazarus grinned and winked at Martha. "Mary said she even promised me she would never nag me about helping her again if I would only get well." He paused again, looking more serious. Quietly, almost in a whisper, the words were found. "Jesus didn't come. And the breath of life left me."

Leah's eyes sparkled with amazement and fear. She shivered and Sarah held her close. "Why didn't Jesus come when he knew you were so sick? Was he busy healing other sick people?"

The disciples were with Jesus when the message came. James knew that side of the story. They arrived with Jesus four days too late to help Lazarus. "Yes, Leah, Jesus was busy healing other people," he said, "but he also deliberately waited."

"Why?" she asked. "He didn't want Lazarus to be sick and die, did he?"

"Well, yes and no," said James, not quite sure how to answer a little girl's grown-up question. "Jesus didn't want Lazarus to suffer. He didn't want anyone to suffer, but he knew Lazarus would die. A few days after receiving the message, he said we needed to go to Bethany because Lazarus was sleeping – that was the word he used. Peter asked him why put us all in danger if Lazarus was sleeping? After all, if he was sleeping, that meant he was recovering. We were all baffled by that one." James glanced toward his brother, who was nodding in agreement.

"It was a mystery to me why he felt such an urgent need to see a man who, by the time we would get there, would be well," John responded.

James continued. "We asked Jesus why. He told us Lazarus was dead and he was glad. We were astounded. Lazarus was his dearest friend. We were too shocked to even ask what he meant, but he knew us well and tried to explain. He was not glad because he wouldn't see his friend again, but because it would give him the opportunity to glorify God in a new way."

"That's right," added John. "When he said Lazarus was dead, it was even more perplexing. Why would he expose us all to danger when he could do nothing except comfort the sisters? We decided he wanted to go and console Mary and Martha because of his long friendship. Whatever his reason, we knew we were going to Bethany – danger or not. His mind was set."

"Jesus knew what he was going to do, didn't he?" asked Leah.

"Yes," replied Lazarus. "Jesus knew, but no one else did. When Martha had sent for him earlier, he responded it was impossible for him to come at that time. She knew the danger to all of them, so she didn't know if he would even be able to make it at all. She hoped and believed he would be there soon. He had once raised a little girl from death, so she had hope for me. He had raised the child within hours of her death, so her hope dimmed with each passing day. Because of the heat, she dared not wait for Jesus. I was rubbed with ointments, wrapped with strips of cloths and laid in the tomb."

Lazarus tried to speak in a casual and matter-of-fact manner, but he could not keep a slight tremble from his voice. He hesitated – whether in fear, excitement, or simply the awareness of all that had happened, even he wasn't sure.

Leah asked very quietly, almost in a whisper, "Were you scared? Wasn't it dark in there? Did you know where you were?"

"I didn't know anything. It was as if I were sound asleep."

"If you were dead, how come you're here? Did Jesus come and make you alive again?" The fear changed to a mixture of awe and doubt.

Lazarus laughed. "Yes, Leah, Jesus came and made me alive again, but not until he had prepared the time and the people. You see, with Jesus timing is everything. Remember he told me when the time was right I would help him with something important."

Lazarus glanced at Mary and Martha, who were lost in their individual thoughts. Martha looked a little pale, almost as if she were reliving that day. Mary, too, hastily wiped away the tears. She didn't want to think about those days, especially since they were replaced by the joy of Lazarus' recovery. Now, however, another grief had again stolen her joy. None of them could understand how Jesus could bring Lazarus back and yet not be able to prevent his own death.

Lazarus continued his story softly and thoughtfully. "My sisters said they were still surrounded by the mourners when someone came to Martha and told her that Jesus was there asking for her. She jumped up and ran to meet him. No one followed her. They were accustomed to Martha rushing out to do something. Typical of Martha, she blamed Jesus. 'If you had come when we sent for you, Lazarus would still be living.'" Martha looked embarrassed but said nothing, and Lazarus continued.

"Jesus reminded her of his teachings about the resurrection, but she misunderstood his words. She ran back to tell Mary, who immediately ran out to meet him. This time the mourners followed because Mary didn't usually act so hastily. Since they thought she was going to the tomb to mourn, they were surprised when she went to meet Jesus instead. Mary was overjoyed to see him, but she also said, 'If only you had come earlier, Lazarus would still be a live.'"

Mary and Martha both bowed their heads, ashamed of their actions even yet. They should have known, and yet how could they?

"I bet Jesus understood them," said Leah. "Jesus understood everyone."

The two women looked at each other, surprised by the child's direct honesty and simplicity. Then they turned and flashed a grateful smile to her.

"Yes," said Lazarus. "Jesus understood, but he still had a lesson for the people to learn. He asked where they had laid me and they told him. 'Come, let us go to him,' he said. Everyone went to the tomb – Mary, Martha, the mourners, the disciples, and the crowds, including some Scribes and Pharisees. They even said Jesus wept for me."

Lazarus paused to wipe his own tears. "Knowing Jesus, I'm not sure he wept for me, because he knew what he would do. I think he wept over the lost condition and confusion of his people."

Lazarus chuckled softly. "Sometimes Jesus had a flare for the spectacular. He had promised me I would be used in an unusual way, but never in my wildest dreams, or nightmares, would I have expected anything like the performance I played that day.

"As I said, with Jesus timing is everything. I wish I could have witnessed that scene before I came out of the tomb. All those people standing there, watching Jesus, wondering if this time he had gone too far. What did he think he could do?

"When he was sure all their attention was focused on him, he prayed, giving thanks for what God was going to do. His whole purpose was to help people believe that God has power even over death.

"Jesus then instructed them to remove the stone. And dear, practical Martha said what everyone must have been thinking." Lazarus teasingly smiled at his sister, then broke into a laugh as she covered her face with her hands. "She said, 'But Lord, it's been four days! The body is decaying. He will stink!'" Lazarus held his nose and made a gagging sound, which ended with more laughing.

Leah giggled even though she did not fully understand. Mary and Martha only shook their heads helplessly at him. He was alive and with them, so they welcomed his teasing and joking.

Getting his laughter under control, Lazarus continued. "Jesus only smiled at her and I heard him call, 'Lazarus. Come out.' I felt a little baffled and I couldn't understand why I was so stiff. I wondered why Jesus was there when I had specifically told my sisters not to call him. The smell of perfume was so strong that I thought Mary must have dropped a bottle of it on me. It was good to hear his voice, though, so I got up to go greet my friend. I felt strangely awkward."

Turning to Leah, Lazarus tried to answer her earlier question. "That's when I noticed the dark, Leah – and a coolness that somehow didn't belong in my room at home. I thought maybe Jesus came after nightfall because of the threats to his life. I felt a rush of fresh air, and the filtered light almost blinded me. Then I was really confused. I thought, If it's night, what is that light? And why is everything so fuzzy? I think I can really understand how Joshua felt when he first received sight."

Joshua smiled and Lazarus continued, "There was a lot of noise and confusion. And then, dead silence."

Lazarus shrugged his shoulders and raised his hands as if giving up. He struggled for words to explain. How do you explain death to persons who have not experienced it? And more to the point, how do you explain returning to life from the depths of death itself?

Even though he felt words were inadequate, Lazarus continued searching for some that could be understood. "Something seemed to be wrapped around me, making it difficult to move." He made a circular motion with his hands indicating how the shroud was wrapped round and round his body. Passing a hand in front of his face, he said, "Even my face was covered so that I couldn't see anything. I was stumbling, trying to get to him. Because I was moving in slow motion, I thought maybe I was dreaming. Then Jesus broke the silence. 'Loose him. Set him free,' he called out. I wondered what he was talking about. I felt hands tearing cloth from my face, then I saw Mary and felt her tears as she tried to free my hands.

"Her hands were trembling so hard I thought she would tie more knots than she untied. Martha joined her. Between the two of them, they managed to free my hands and I could help with the rest. I couldn't understand why they kept crying, and why everyone else stood like stone statues. Then I saw Jesus. He simply smiled and winked at me conspiratorially. It was then I knew what my special service to him would be – or rather, was."

Lazarus laughed. "'Do you want to drown me?' I asked as I held my sisters close to me. I could only guess at what anguish they had been through and for how long. I didn't know how long I had been in that grave.

"'What's going on here anyway?' I asked. No one could, or would, say anything. Mary and Martha just cried, and Jesus stood there smiling at us. 'Well, if no one wants to say anything, I guess that's all right,' I said, 'but I wish you would do something to get rid of this odor. I smell like a perfume shop.' I couldn't understand why someone didn't say something."

"What could we say?" asked Mary. "There simply were no words to describe what a person feels when someone they loved was dead and lives again."

Lazarus chuckled. "I guess you're right. When I was finally loose and felt my muscles move again, I also felt a rumbling inside me. I realized it had been several days since I had eaten, so I said, 'I'm hungry. Jesus is here. Let's have a feast.' Poor Martha, that was too much for her," he said as he flashed a smile at her which she returned. "She gave me an odd look – kind of a cross between exasperation, joy, and an 'I-can't-believe-he-said-that' look. She tried to sound stern as she answered me. 'You've been dead four days. We cried, scolded Jesus, and set the town on end, and all you can say is you're hungry!'

"I couldn't believe what she was saying. Dead four days? How could I have been dead four days? Surely she was mistaken, or just kidding me. Then I looked into the eyes of my friend, Jesus, and I knew what a really special plan he'd had for me. Not only did he raise me from death, but he was showing us God's ultimate power over even death."

Lazarus paused and looked around the room at each one who had told their story before him, and others who were still waiting. As the tears of joy ran unashamedly down his face, he said, "Martha, Mary, Jesus and so many friends – we all wept together for joy and went home to talk and eat."

Leah giggled. "What did you eat? Did you really have a party?"

"Oh, yes," said Lazarus. "We had a real feast. Folks had brought food for the mourning sisters. Martha got busy and fixed more. We had the best feast ever."

"That makes me hungry," she said. "Can I have something now?" She looked up at Sarah and then to her mother. Before Sarah could move, Adam was on his feet and moving toward the table.

Lazarus rose from his chair and moved toward Peter, who was still seated, nervously picking at threads of his tunic. Lazarus stood before him, his hands resting on Peter's drooped shoulders. "Peter, God called me back from death to life, not because life is better than death, but to help us poor mortals understand the power of God. And as I said before, it's all in the timing. If God loved me enough to do this great miracle, could he not do the same for his own Son, Jesus?"

Peter, his head back so he could look into his friend's eyes, stared unblinking, unasked questions in his eyes and on his lips.

Lazarus continued, "Yes, Peter, you know I was there. I couldn't have stayed away. I witnessed his death. And I believe I shall witness his life. I was gone four days. It has been almost three days now since his death. Jesus was my closest friend. He found joy and contentment in little things. He looked for ways to surprise and give joy to me and to everyone that he knew. Look for the sunrise, Peter. Who knows? It may bring a surprise or two."

Lazarus stood a moment longer, looking into the troubled eyes of his friend. Then, giving him a friendly squeeze on the shoulders, he moved back to the table where he filled his cup and joined his sisters in a darkened corner of the room.

Chapter Ten

Let the Children Come

Peter stared unblinking at the empty spot where Lazarus had stood. Across the room someone sighed deeply – a long intake and slow exhaling of air. Echoes of so many words reverberated in the recesses of minds already overloaded with unanswered questions and anxious hopes. Stirring from his motionless stance, Peter combed his fingers through his wild straggly hair, stood, stretched, and moved to the now-familiar spot by the window. Lazarus had given him much to think about.

He tried to sort out and make sense of all he heard. The words of Lazarus especially made him rethink the past and the future. *It was true Lazarus was dead four days when Jesus raised him to life again. And Jesus did say earlier he would have to die and be raised again. We didn't want to believe him then, but now...* The thought was left hanging. His mind was too full. He thought he could contain no more words or thoughts.

The sound of footsteps softly approached the table. Peter turned to face the youth who, having satisfied his young sister's appetite, returned to the table to get something for himself. Adam moved as noiselessly as he could. It was not his purpose to draw attention to himself. However, Peter sought release for pent-up feelings. Pointing an accusing finger at the boy, as he had done to others earlier, Peter snapped like a dog whose turf had been invaded. "You're only a child. Surely you didn't witness the events of the last few days." Peter knew better, even as he had with others before him. He saw the youth with his father standing nearer to the cross than he himself dared to stand.

Adam stopped, holding a piece of cheese mid-way to his mouth. He fixed his gaze on Peter, his own trembling emotions begging for control. "Yes, sir, I was there." Adam gulped to swallow a wave of fear and awe of this gruff, angry disciple. "And excuse me, but I am not a child!" His tone defied anyone to contradict him. "I am almost fourteen. I loved Jesus very much. He was my friend." He trembled slightly, but refused to back down.

"Your friend? What do you know about friendship? Children shouldn't have any part in the adult world of grief!" Pausing, Peter reflected, *Adults shouldn't have to be here either.*

"Excuse me, sir," said the young man, gaining courage by Peter's lack of control, "but you don't seem to have changed your mind much about children. I remember a couple of years ago when Jesus was teaching in our village. We heard he was there and persuaded our parents to take us to hear the great teacher."

The boy's words brought him out of his morose. Peter stared at the youth. *How can he speak to me like that? It's bad enough the little girl speaks so boldly, but this young man dares to speak to me as if we are equals!*

Before Peter could express his thoughts, however, Adam continued, still standing by the table holding his snack. "We were excited, so we probably did make a lot of noise. But we just wanted to be near Jesus – to touch him – to know he was real. My little sister, Leah, wanted to sit on his lap and touch his beard."

Adam stood pressing his piece of cheese between his fingers, but he rushed on, afraid he would lose his nerve if he stopped talking. "You and the others told us to go away," he said accusingly. "You said we were making too much noise and the teacher was busy with more important matters. Leah started to cry when we told her we had to leave. She was only four and didn't understand adults. We were leaving when Jesus called to us and motioned for us to come to him. He told you to let us come to him.[1] We ran to him before anyone could stop us. He took Leah on his lap and I stood beside him. He put an arm around me and I felt like I was a real person – someone important. I was just a kid then, but those things were important to me."

Adam hastily brushed away the tears that threatened to spill over his glaring eyes. He popped the much softened cheese into his mouth and gulped hard to swallow it.

Peter remembered the incident very well and would have commented, but Adam turned from his gaze and continued talking. He, like the others, needed to share his feelings and his story to keep his own memories fresh and alive.

"I think Jesus could read my thoughts. He told me I was very important to him. Then he turned to the people who were all around us and said, 'You need to become like these little children if you want to see the Kingdom of God.'

"I didn't understand what he meant, but I don't think a lot of the adults did either. I felt proud to be a child that day." Adam began to feel a little awkward and self-conscious standing by the table. He picked up his cup, filled it, took another piece of cheese and some bread and returned to his seat by his parents. Peter stood glued to the spot. Before he could think of anything to say, Adam, feeling the safety of his parents nearby, spoke again.

"I liked to sleep on the roof with my straw mat – like Jesus and Lazarus. That night I felt like I could almost touch the stars. I tried to count them, but gave up. They seemed to keep multiplying. I remembered God's promise to Father Abraham. His descendants would number more than the stars.[2] And I remembered Jesus saying people are more important than even sparrows and lilies. I wondered if we were also more precious than those beautiful stars. A breeze whispered in the trees and I could almost hear the words of the prophet Isaiah when he said we are precious in God's sight and he loves us."[3]

Adam paused and glanced around the room for encouragement. Nods and murmurs around the room gave him courage. Lazarus spoke what they all thought. "You're right, Adam. The prophets reminded us over and over how much God loves us."

Adam appreciated the smile Lazarus gave him, and his own flushed face slipped into a smile of gratitude. With more confidence, he courageously gave voice to his own inward musings. "Jesus said so many things I didn't understand. I tried to imagine what he meant about children and the Kingdom of God. I could picture a kingdom where all the leaders were kids. Somehow, I didn't really think that's what he meant. There had to be more to being a leader than simply being a child. Surely grown-ups would have more knowledge, but did they have important things like love...trust...and joy?

"My mind was overflowing with questions about grown-ups and their lack of trust. Most of the time they seem to be anxious, worried, and concerned about something – anything, it seems, will do. It's almost unheard of to smile in the Temple or Synagogue, or to let someone important to you know they are loved – especially someone who's not a part of your family." Adam's frown indicated the thoughts still troubled him.

Mary smiled, then glancing from Adam to her brother, Lazarus, and back to Adam, she said, "You sound like Lazarus when he was your age. He used to grumble to Martha and me every time he came back from worship. 'Everything is so serious,' he used to say, 'everything, that is, except people's commitment to God.' Do you remember how you used to complain, Lazarus?" She turned to face her brother.

"I remember," he said, smiling at his sister.

Taking a drink of water, Adam turned to face more of the people. He continued thoughtfully, measuring his words as he spoke. "What Peter says is true, I suppose. I am hardly more than a child in terms of years. But meeting Jesus, getting to know him, and then watching him die caused something to happen inside." Adam laid his hand on his chest as he spoke.

"I feel much older. I have become a man, even though the years are few." Adam's eyes filled with tears again and his voice cracked. Angrily he brushed aside the tears. *But real men don't cry*, he thought.

"Tell us your story, Adam," encouraged Lazarus. He had compassion and understanding for this young man who was, as he said, hardly more than a child. And yet, he sensed there was indeed a story which should be added to the collective memory of Jesus.

Adam glanced at Peter, expecting him to object, but Peter mumbled something that sounded like, "Go ahead."

Adam took a deep breath. "Thank you," he said with gratitude. "I think I need to hear it myself. Sometimes I wonder if all that's happened is really true. Have I really seen and heard what I think I have?" He took a sip from his glass, needing time to collect his thoughts. "The Torah means a lot to me. Even before I met Jesus, I hoped to become a rabbi. Now, I am not sure."

Lazarus nodded, understanding perfectly the battle raging within the young man. How can a person feel so strongly about following God and yet have such doubts concerning the institution which proclaims that God? Yes, Lazarus understood the boy's struggles. He had been there.

Adam sensed this kindred spirit in Lazarus and was grateful. "The Prophet Isaiah's words raised more questions in my mind – questions about God's love and how God knows us each one by name. What did Jesus mean by becoming as children? Even I knew a person can't be born all over again and become a child again." Adam grinned at Nicodemus, who smiled in return.

"I tried to figure it all out. Maybe he meant we need to smile more, hug more, worry less, and be happy. Most children don't worry about food, clothes, or a place to sleep. Our parents provide all of that. Since Jesus called God his Father, and all of us his brothers and sisters, does that mean that God is our Father and takes care of our food, clothes, and a place to sleep? I like to think so. The more I thought about these kinds of things, the more I didn't want to ever grow up. I hoped I would always trust God the way I did that night."

John watched the young fisherman intently. *It's unusual for one so young to have such a searching mind*, he thought. *I must talk with him later*. Adam, unaware of John's scrutiny, hesitated, then continued with a touch of sadness in his voice. "But I did start to grow up. No one can hold back the sands of time.

"Then one day I saw Jesus again. My father allowed me to join the crowds where he was preaching near the cove. Our boat was docked there for some minor repairs. I listened all day. He told fascinating stories and gave practical advice for living. I had been so intent I hadn't realized how late it was getting, until the sun sank lower to the horizon. I couldn't believe the day was nearly gone. People started to murmur about being hungry and having a long way to travel to get home."

Adam turned to face Peter. "The disciples must have heard them too. I heard you say, 'But Master, it's getting late. We have to send them on their way.' And Jesus answered, 'We can't send them home this late in the day without food. Many have traveled a great distance. Feed them.'"[4]

Adam laughed. It was a joyful sound of genuine amusement, not harsh with grown-up cynicism. "I will never forget the look on your face when he said, 'Feed them.' I had to laugh. You scowled at me, but Andrew came over and asked if I would like to help him get the people organized in groups on the hillside. It was a dream come true for me. I was actually doing something to help Jesus! I offered him my lunch. I had been so absorbed in his words I forgot to eat. I didn't know how it could help, but it was all I had and I wanted Jesus to have it."

"That's when Jesus multiplied it," said Leah. "Adam told me Jesus took his lunch and..."

"Leah!" her father, who had been very quiet, cut her off rather sharply. "It's Adam's story. Let him tell it."

"I'm sorry," she said, truly repentant, but also giving the impression of knowing her father did not waste words. When he spoke, she listened.

Adam smiled at her. "Thank you, Leah. That's the best part of the story. I certainly don't want to leave it out."

He then turned his concentration back to that day near the beach. "Andrew took my lunch to Jesus, who was happy to get it. He fed everyone with it! There was even food left over to give to the poor." Adam's eyes grew wide and his voice showed the awe that he still felt as the memories flooded his consciousness.

Andrew nodded and smiled at Adam. "I remember," he said. "You had only five barley cakes and two fish. We had no idea what Jesus could do with such a small amount. But, as he took them, he smiled and winked at us the way he used to do when he was about to share some joke or surprise with us. He told us to get the people seated in groups of fifty."

"That was sure fun!" Adam had to laugh as he remembered the scene. "Some folks didn't want to listen to us. Some figured they knew a better way. Some were sarcastic, wanting to know if God was going to send manna, but most were willing to cooperate and we soon had them in groups. There must have been five thousand or more folks there that day!"

Adam raised his hands as he had seen Jesus do. "Jesus raised his hands like this, and it was so quiet we could hear the water lapping at the sands of the distant shore. Even the squawking birds by the sea seemed to stop their shrieking because those hands were raised."

Andrew loved the story as much as Adam did. He couldn't help interjecting his thoughts. "Then Jesus blessed the food and began breaking it into portions. We brought one person – as a kind of steward – from each group and more or less got them in twelve lines. Jesus broke the fish and bread, gave a portion to each of us disciples, who then gave it to the stewards of each group. They in turn gave it to each one in their group of fifty."

"I couldn't believe how it multiplied," Adam continued, picking up the story with renewed excitement. He didn't mind at all that Andrew had joined him. It seemed so natural. "Can you believe we actually fed over five thousand men, women and children that day? Jesus sat on a large boulder, smiling like...like..." He searched his young mind for the right and proper word. Finally he said, "Like my father did when he saw me catch my first fish."

Adam beamed. "I thought my eyes were playing tricks on me. He just kept breaking the bread and then the fish, and they just kept multiplying. I think it tasted better than any bread and fish I ever ate, even better than that first fish I caught so long ago."

Adam paused and stared with Mary into the darkness of the night. Somewhere in the dark streets of Jerusalem, a dog yelped, followed by an angry man's voice. Adam shivered and slowly turned his gaze back to the candlelight and comfort of the room. His voice became a little softer as he continued his story. "While I ate that feast of bread and fish, I couldn't help but notice the hungry and sometimes uncaring people who sat on the ground around the gentle, smiling Messiah. It seemed so out of balance. And again I remembered his words about becoming children. I wondered if becoming like children had something to do with loving him enough to give him all we have and receiving all he wants to give.

"I wanted to stay with Jesus and become one of his disciples. I thought maybe I could simply be a helper or something. You know, care for his needs like the boys in a king's palace. I'm sure King David had boys in his court. I'm not sure what they were called. I was about to ask him if I could stay, but the disciples all got in the boat and set out to sea. Jesus turned toward the mountain and walked quickly, as if he was late for a very special meeting. I guessed he wanted to talk to his Father, so I returned to mine. There would be another time and we had work to do before the next day's fishing."

"Multiplying the food wasn't the only miracle of that night," spoke Thaddeus. He was one of the quieter disciples. Adam's words had pricked his memory. They all were awed by the way Jesus fed the people from only a small lunch. The remembrance triggered other memories of that night.

Thaddeus spoke softly for a big man. "After the people had been refreshed with the fish and bread, they began to disappear almost as quickly as they had appeared. They needed to get back to their homes before dark. It had been a long day, as Adam said, and we were all tired and wanted to rest. We thought surely Jesus was tired, too. But you were very perceptive, Adam. He did want to go pray. So he told us to get in our boat and cross over to the other side of the sea. He said he was going to pray and would meet us later.

"We didn't argue. We just got in the boat and divided the chores of running it. Some of us settled down to sleep until our turn to keep watch. It didn't occur to us to wonder about how Jesus would catch up with us. Several hours later, I was awake for my turn to keep the boat going.

"We were somewhere toward the middle of the Sea of Galilee. As I watched, I walked slowly around the boat. I was startled by what seemed to be a man approaching us.[5] I knew that was impossible. We were in the middle of the sea, but it sure looked like someone was walking on the water! I thought it must be a trick of the mist rising from the sea. I woke the others. We all watched the form draw nearer. The closer it got to the boat the more it looked like a man. We all knew men don't walk on water. The sea was certainly too deep out there to be walking on the bottom of it. To say we were frightened is putting it mildly!"

Thaddeus laughed as the scene became vivid in his mind. "Oh, I can laugh now," he said, "but I had to clench my teeth together to keep from screaming then."

"I remember," laughed Nathaniel. "We were all scared out of our wits."

"Seeing that form of a man moving toward us, gliding along on the water like it was solid, was scary enough," added Thaddeus, "but when the form spoke, we all would have fainted dead away if there hadn't been something familiar about the man that kept us watching. 'Don't be afraid. It is I,' he said to us across the waves."

"You're right when you say we were all frightened," said Philip. "We knew it sounded like Jesus, but it was so hard to believe. We had left him on shore, heading toward the mountain to pray. How could he be in the middle of the sea?"

Thaddeus continued grinning as he glanced at Thomas. "Usually Thomas is the first one to raise doubts and questions, but that time it was Peter who said, 'If it is really you, let me come to you.' We all looked at him like he had taken leave of his senses. The water was very deep. Peter is a good swimmer, but still...Well, we didn't know for sure it was Jesus, and Peter was taking an awful chance."

"Why didn't you know it was Jesus?" asked Leah. "Didn't you know the sound of his voice, like Joshua?"

"Normally we would," said Nathaniel. "But when you're frightened and in a place you don't expect someone, it makes things sound different."

"I guess Jesus surprised you, huh?"

"He certainly did."

"Did Peter jump overboard and swim out to see if it was Jesus?" she asked.

"Jesus told Peter to come to him. We all held our breath as Peter stepped over the side of the boat into the water. We were amazed as he took a few steps, almost like the water had suddenly turned solid under his feet. Actually, he was doing quite well until he remembered he couldn't do that."

"You mean he was walking on top of the water?" Leah looked at Peter with a new kind of awe and respect.

"He did until he remembered people can't do that. Then he started sinking." Thaddeus laughed. The others joined him.

"Well, I didn't see any of the rest of you even try it," said Peter, glaring at them.

"No, we were too scared," said Nathaniel as he wiped the tears of mirth from his eyes. He tried to look serious. "We were all so afraid we felt glued to the boat."

"It was Jesus and he got Peter back into the boat. The next thing we knew, we were at our destination," Thaddeus said. "But I'm sorry Adam," he apologized. "I didn't mean to take your story. What happened after you left us?"

Adam smiled. "That was neat. I wish I could have been there."

"Me too." Leah loved the water and would like any occasion to play in it.

"I'm sure you would," said her brother, who had more than once pulled her from the sea.

"When I got back to our boat, I was really excited. I told my father what Jesus had done and I wanted to be just like him someday. My father looked a little sad. I'm sure he was thinking more in terms of losing a partner. Then I asked him if he thought Jesus was the Messiah."

Adam glanced at his father as he continued, "'Of course not,' he answered. 'The Messiah will be a King. That man is a prophet, maybe, but certainly not the Messiah.'"

Saul coughed. He was not used to being talked about in this way, especially by his son, and yet, he was proud of Adam and the way he was taking a stand. "I still think the man was a prophet," he said in his low, gruff voice. "Surely, if he was the Messiah, we would not be gathered here this night, grieving his death."

Adam smiled in embarrassment. "Sometimes my father and I don't agree, but I'm grateful that he allows me the freedom to disagree with him and to think for myself. And I can't ever express enough thanks that he is here with me tonight, even though he may not believe as completely as I do."

Adam lifted his cup to his lips and took a sip. Taking a deep breath, he continued his story. "I didn't see Jesus again until last week. I didn't forget him or my desire to be like him. Our family came down to Jerusalem from Galilee early for Passover. Our caravan set up camp just outside Jerusalem, since we don't have relatives in the city. One afternoon Leah ran into the tent and said she heard Jesus was coming this way. We gathered all the children in the camp to go see him. I wanted them all to have the same thrill I experienced the first time I met him."

"That was fun," said Leah, clapping her hands together. "We ran to all my friends and got them to go. Sophie's mother wasn't going to let her go. But when she knew Adam was taking us, she said it was all right. That's because Adam is honest and people trust him and... " Leah stopped mid-sentence. Her brother was staring at her with a funny mixture of mirth and sternness.

"Oops! Sorry," Leah said, clasping her hands over her mouth.

A small ripple of laughter went around the room. Adam smiled at his sister, shook his head, and returned to his narrative. "It was fun being with the kids. We went to the gate of the city where we could see Jesus coming. On our way I told them Jesus was an important teacher – maybe even the Messiah.

"It was amazing how quickly they understood. A wave of sadness suddenly swept over me as I realized I had already lost my childish way of catching the excitement. One little fellow, who was about four or five years old, suggested that we should wave palm branches.

'Because my dad says that means honor for a King,' he said. It was a great idea! I was just sorry I hadn't thought of it myself! With tireless enthusiasm they gathered palm branches and ran to meet Jesus, waving them wildly and shouting, 'Hosanna! Hosanna!'[6]

"Pretty soon a crowd gathered and the children's liveliness was contagious. Everyone began shouting and waving branches. Some even laid their coats on the road to make a royal path for the little donkey on which Jesus rode." Adam paused and added, "Then some big guy started laughing." Trying to mimic the man, Adam said, "'Look at that man on the donkey,' he said. 'He sure don't look like no king to me! Kings ride white horses and dress in fancy clothes.' He laughed an ugly kind of laugh again...so I...eh...kicked him." Adam looked sheepish, and added, "Then I ran."

Leah put her hands over her mouth again, this time to hide the giggle. Her brother glared at her, but she couldn't help herself. She laughed out loud and everyone joined her. "It did look pretty funny when you kicked that big guy. He yelled a lot of words that Mom says I shouldn't hear."

There was a gasp from Miriam.

"Whoops," said Leah. "I wasn't supposed to let her know I heard them."

It was impossible to hide the laughter and sense of joy that seemed to be slowly replacing the grief. How strange it felt to be gathered for a night of grieving, and yet feel such contentment, and even joy. Was it the child's presence? Again they could almost hear Jesus saying, "A little child shall lead them..."

"It was a pretty funny-looking sight when you think about it – Jesus sitting on that silly little donkey." John smiled as he remembered Jesus on the little donkey. "But that's the way he was. Certainly not silly, but he took every opportunity to remind us of how often we take life far too seriously. The man was right. A white horse and all the pomp and circumstance signal leadership to us, but God sees things differently. Jesus was sort of making fun of a system that defines a person by their looks or actions."

"Well," said Peter bitterly. "It looks like the system had the last laugh, didn't it?"

"Did it?" asked John, glancing at Lazarus. "I'm not so sure about that anymore."

Peter was perplexed. He opened his mouth to say more, but Adam had continued talking, so he closed it and leaned against the window frame and listened.

"I heard some of the leaders from the Temple tell Jesus to make the kids keep quiet and go home. Jesus told them if every one of us were to keep silent, the very stones would cry out.[7] They thought he was crazy. He looked at me and winked. I winked back. From somewhere deep within me came knowledge, and I knew what he meant. The crunching of the little donkey's feet on the stones and the whisper of the palm leaves would speak out like the Psalms tell us. If we had not been there, God would have provided the music for the procession.

"I began to catch the old excitement – excitement like the little ones. We followed him up the hill. Jesus stopped and looked out over the city. From that point you can see almost all of Jerusalem. Even in the midst of the beauty of the city, I will never forget the sad look on his face. Even the cross did not bring such a look of pain."

Adam paused. A grimace crossed his own face. "I saw the tears roll down his face and heard him say, 'O Jerusalem, Jerusalem. How I loved you and tried to make you understand. I wanted to love you and protect you but you wouldn't let me.'[8]

"Then he just shook his head sadly and started toward Jerusalem. I felt helpless. I wanted to do something, but didn't know what. He glanced at me as if he had read my thoughts. I was a little embarrassed, and somehow a little more of the child in me died. I wanted to turn and run."

Mary turned back to face the young man. She spoke with a voice full of compassion. "It hurts very much to lose something, or someone, dear to your heart. Jesus loved Jerusalem – not just the buildings within the city walls, but the people. He loved all the people, who for centuries turned their backs on God. He used to talk about how much he wished they had listened to Jeremiah and the other prophets, and had returned to God. Growing up is full of pain; however, it is also full of love. Don't ever forget that. You were a source of comfort to Jesus in his time of need. You will be a greater source of help in years to come."

Adam smiled at her, swiping the back of his hand across his eyes. "Thank you," he replied. For the first time he felt being an adult was not so painful.

Adam took a gulp from his cup. He looked around the room, momentarily resting his eyes on Peter. Then his gaze searched out his parents where he found encouragement to move on with the words that begged to be spoken. His voice was soft and etched with pain. "A few days ago I heard a lot of commotion and thought Jesus was leading another parade. Something prompted me to run and see what was happening before I gathered the children. I'm glad I did."

Adam gave an involuntary shudder, took a deep breath and proceeded. "Jesus was leading another parade, all right, but this time he was not even riding a silly little donkey. He was walking – or I should say, stumbling – with much difficulty. Across his shoulder and dragging behind him was a big cross, which he lugged down the street and up the steps to the hill of the Skull. I could not keep the cry from my lips as I ran to him. He stumbled and fell. I reached to help him up, but one of the soldiers kicked me away. I was so angry and confused I hardly felt the pain which shot through my leg as his swift kick made contact.

"As I fell, I felt the rough cobblestone tear open the thin layer of flesh over my eye. The warm flow of blood down my face, mocked my desire to help. Through my tears of anger and frustration I saw the soldiers pull a big, dark-skinned man from the crowd.[9] They made him help Jesus, who lifted his head slightly as he tried to lift his body up. His blood-soaked eyes met mine as we lay almost face to face on the ground. I think he even tried to smile at me."

Adam had to pause to gain control of his choking, trembling voice. Taking several deep breaths, he lifted his face toward the ceiling where no eyes could stare back at him. His voice, more or less under control, he pushed on, a slight smile playing at the corners of his mouth.

"I believe he would have winked at me if his eyes had not been so swollen. Somewhere deep down inside me I heard his words from what seemed so long ago, 'Let the children come to me.' At that moment in the depths of my heart I vowed that I would go every step of the way with him. Nothing could have stopped me. Nothing."

Adam paused and glanced at his father with a mixture of love, respect and awe. He turned his gaze to a safe place – the ceiling, his cup, even the table of food. He spoke softly, but clearly. "My father saw me run to watch the parade and followed. I guess he knew from the sound of the crowd it was not a joyous occasion like the one a week earlier. Before I could lift myself off the ground, he was by my side, helping me up. He tore off a piece of his tunic and placed it on the bleeding wound on my head, urging me to come with him back to the camp where we could take care of it properly. I refused. I was angry, humiliated and sad. There was no way I could go to the comfort of even our temporary home while Jesus was heading for Golgotha. I had never spoken to either of my parents in a disrespectful tone, but in my anger and frustration, I yelled at my father as if it was his fault. I told him I was no longer a child and I would go to Golgotha with or without his consent. My father had every right and reason to punish me like a two year old, but he didn't."

Adam's tears flowed unchecked. Smiling at his father through the rainbow created by tears and candlelight, his voice sounded tired and much older than his few years warranted. The words continued to come unrestrained. "Suddenly I felt very old – older even than my grandfather. I knew I would go to Golgotha and I would stay to the end. My father, who should have treated me like a defiant child, put his arms around my shoulder and said, 'Come on. We'll have to hurry to catch up with them.'"

Adam choked back a sob. "Even though I keep declaring I am not a child, I wonder. If it's true, why will the tears not stop flowing? Men don't cry like this."

Saul, the gruff-looking fisherman – tears flowing down his own face – came to the side of his young son, who struggled with his emotions. "Don't they?" he asked. "It's all right, my son. Never be ashamed of your tears. They're not the mark of a child. They're just as often the sign of a compassionate, caring man. You're right. You have aged beyond your years, and Jesus, whether prophet or Messiah, has a lifetime disciple who will be true and faithful forever."

Placing his arms around his son, Saul held him close until the boy/man could once again gain control. With his father's arm still around his shoulders, Adam finished his story as simply as he could. "I went to Golgotha and I watched them crucify him. The soldiers divided his clothes and gambled for them. They offered him vinegar when he said he was thirsty. I heard him say, 'It is finished.'[10] One more part of the child within me died. I cried out to God – whether aloud or in my heart, I don't know. I prayed, 'If this is what grown-ups do to other grown-ups, then...I...I don't ever want to grow up. I want to remain a carefree child forever.' Even though I knew God heard me, I also knew I could not remain a child forever. Oh, yes, I have crossed over the line and can never go back. I am a man, granted a young man."

Turning back to look at Peter, he answered the earlier, harsh question. "Yes, I was there. I watched all that took place. I vowed within my heart to follow Jesus as long and as far as I possibly can – to the grave if necessary. As soon as the first rays of light shatter the darkness of this night, I will go with the rest of you and say goodbye for the last time. Then I will seek out the children, wherever they are, and tell his story again and again and again."

Adam hesitated, his agonized, youthful eyes staring into the dark, troubled eyes of Peter. Then he asked, not with malice, but with empathy, "What about you, Simon Peter, Sir? Where were you? Were you there?"

The young man looked Peter straight in the eyes for a full minute, neither of them speaking, neither of them blinking. Then Adam lowered his gaze and quietly went back to his seat with his father's arm still around him. They sat quietly together. Peter stared after them as if he had been struck by a back-handed blow to the face, Adam's words echoed in his mind. *Were you there? Were...you...there? Were...*

Chapter Eleven

Not Me, Lord!

Peter, eyes blazing, stared speechlessly at the young man who had told such a moving story. Time came to a halt, and he alone was caught in the blur of timelessness. Only the echo of the boy's words gave him a sense of the present. Silence, which followed Adam's words, was suddenly shattered. A loud crash pushed time back on its rightful track, and Peter blinked and turned toward the sound. "What was...?" The question was left unfinished when he saw his brother on his knees beside his chair, picking up pieces of pottery.

"Sorry," murmured Andrew, a sheepish grin creasing his face. "The cup just sort of slipped." He continued cleaning up the mess.

Tension felt as thick as a morning fog. Andrew hadn't dropped the cup intentionally. However, it did take the focus off Peter long enough for him to collect his thoughts.

"Sleeping with your eyes open?" kidded Lazarus, dropping to his knees beside Andrew. "Let me help," he said and began picking up some pieces.

"Here's a sponge to soak up the liquid." Mary knelt beside them and began mopping up the spill.

"Don't we have this backwards?" asked Lazarus. "Martha is the one who does this kind of stuff. You sit and dream. Remember?" The candlelight magnified the twinkle in his eyes, causing them to sparkle even more than usual. Mary lifted the wet sponge and would have thrown it at him if her sister had not snatched it from her hand. Lazarus pretended to duck, laughing at Mary, who covered her mouth to hide her chagrin and shock. *How could I have done such a childish thing? It seems everyone is acting out of character tonight,* she thought. *Is it the grief? The uncertainty? The closeness of mind and spirit?* Meekly she continued to help clean up the broken pieces of cup and the spilled liquid, glad for activity to hide mixed emotions.

Peter, his face still frozen somewhere between shock and pain, knew the dropped cup – accidental, or not – and the teasing were meant to give him time to recover. The boy was right. He had to face the truth. Mary, Martha, Lazarus, Andrew – they all wanted to help him with his struggle, but what could they say? Adam wasn't hateful, just truthful, and it hit too close to the heart of each one's own feelings of inadequacies. Where were they when Jesus needed them most? Could they have done more? Peter knew he was not alone. Every other person in the room seemed to be wrestling and struggling with the same questions.

Running his fingers through his hair and rubbing his temples with his finger tips, Peter tried to push the echo from his mind. *Where were you? Where were you? Where were...* Slowly his feet slipped into his limited back and forth pacing. Very, very slowly he moved. Maybe he could walk the sound away. There were so many questions and so few answers.

Soon the dawn would pull the darkness of the night away and he would have to face the future whether he was ready or not. The words of the young man continued to ring in his ears: *What about you, Simon Peter? Where were you? Were you there?* Peter cupped his hands over his ears to shut out the sound of the voice, but he knew it was a futile action. The voice was no longer in the room. It was bouncing around within the confines of his mind and couldn't be quieted. He sighed deeply as thoughts and words tumbled and raced backward. Slowly he removed his hands from his ears and let them drop to his side. Looking around the room, which seemed unusually quiet, his gaze drifted and lingered momentarily on each who had volunteered a story.

Who would have thought a member of the Sanhedrin would be hiding with us in this time of mourning? And yet, here they are – Nicodemus and Joseph. Nicodemus used the cover of night because of his fear, and now, here he is again under cover of night – this time giving courage to the rest of us.

And there's the Samaritan woman – Sarah, she calls herself, because of her change in attitude. Not only was her life changed, but a whole village is following Jesus because of her faith and belief.

Turning his concentration from Sarah, Peter stared at Joshua, who had been born blind. *The man can now see more clearly than many of us who were born with clear vision.* Joshua, sensing Peter's gaze upon him, met his stare with his own eyes raised. Peter, embarrassed to be caught staring, dropped his head and closed his eyes.

Sighing deeply once again, Peter raised his head and continued to contemplate others. Beside Andrew, Lazarus was picking up the last slivers of the broken cup. His was an incredible and marvelous story of resurrection. Who could, or would, believe it? Peter wanted to believe but... *And what of the young man who has just spoken? He came to Jesus as a child – one of the children I would have turned away from seeing Jesus. And now he's a faithful servant – more faithful than I am.*

Once the mess made by the spilled liquid and broken cup was cleared, Mary and Martha went back to checking on others. Lazarus sat in the chair beside Andrew. They spoke quietly to one another. Around the room, soft murmurs rose and fell as the mourners talked quietly in twos and threes. Leah dozed on Sarah's lap. Miriam offered to take her, but Sarah said she was all right.

Peter continued to scrutinize each one in the room, those who had told their story, and those who had not – drawing them into his thoughts as if they could somehow push his painful memories aside. *Each one of them had a story to tell because Jesus had entered and changed their lives. Most of them were at the cross*, thought Peter. *And the boy was right. What about me – Peter the Rock? Where was I? Oh, I was there all right, but...* Try as he would to push aside painful memories, they kept returning with increasing frequency – jabbing, pounding, poking at his already beleaguered mind. Peter glanced toward the window, cocking his head to one side. He stood motionless.

"Are you all right, Peter?" Thomas moved toward the door to check outside. "You look a little pale."

"What?" Peter looked surprised to see someone there, once again lost in that timelessness. He brushed his hand across his face. "Oh, no...no...I'm all right. I just...thought I heard something."

"I'll check," said Thomas and opened the doors so softly that most did not even notice he had done so. *He won't find anything*, thought Peter. *I was so sure I heard a rooster crowing somewhere in the distance, but that, too, is only an echo of past.* Memories were deluging faster than he could to deal with them.

Thomas returned as quietly as he had left. No one had really noticed the exchange between the two men. "There's no one around," he told Peter. "Everything seems quiet. You can almost smell the dawn coming. Stars are beginning to fade."

"Thanks, Thomas. I didn't think anyone was there," said Peter. "I guess we're all getting jumpy. We need sleep, but..." The words were left hanging. There was no need to finish the sentence. They both knew it would be impossible to sleep until the whole matter was put to rest.

Having lost some of his agitation, Peter was almost calm as he began to speak, his voice soft, barely above a whisper. Those farthest from him strained to hear his words. Murmuring and whispering ceased. Somehow it was a different Peter speaking – less agitated and angry – more calm and resigned. They all knew Peter had a lot of stories to tell, and that he was wrestling with more than mere grief. It was only a matter of time until he would be able to share. Maybe the time was now.

"It seems like a lifetime ago when I first met Jesus," he began, glancing around the room. "We had been friends a long time. Even as a young man, I was impressed by him. He was always so confident and sure of himself, no matter what he was doing. I was just the opposite, quick and impulsive and yet uncertain."

Peter half-laughed in spite of his anxious, sorrowful feelings. "Even his appearance impressed me! For a carpenter he was always neat. His hair and beard always seemed to stay in place."

Unconsciously he stroked his own rough, shaggy beard and ran his fingers through his wild, fly-away hair as if the action would separate his thoughts. He turned to the window, his back to the room.

Clearing his throat, he turned again, facing the room full of friends. Gaining a little more confidence from the stories which had been shared, his voice gained volume. "We talked many times about the day when he would be something other than a carpenter."

Talking and walking at the same time, Peter moved toward Mary, the mother of Jesus. He stopped near her and smiled. She lifted her smiling face in return. He knew she loved to hear stories of Jesus, and especially about the time before he left home. He squeezed her lovingly on the shoulder and turned taking a few steps back toward the door.

"Jesus was an excellent carpenter. Business was good. Satisfied customers would send others to him. I didn't understand why he would want to give it up. I'm sure it wasn't the money. He was more interested in people being satisfied than he was in making a living.

"I used to ask him why he wanted to give it up. I told him he could become very wealthy if he would just charge more and insist that people pay when they pick up the article. Always in that patient tone, which sometimes infuriated me, he would tell me God had other plans. And I would ask him, 'Then why wait? Why not now?' He would laugh and say God would work in God's own time. I was impatient. It seemed God moved so slowly – for whatever it was he wanted Jesus to do. If I had only known, I wouldn't have been so impatient for time to move on. If only I had known." His voice once again dropped to almost a whisper as he turned his back and moved toward the window.

Pausing to take in all the signs of the quickly speeding night, Peter again took a deep breath, swallowing it as if the air had become very thick and heavy. Time now was moving too quickly. When did it speed up? He turned toward the table.

"Not long after the baptism and the time in the wilderness, which we heard about earlier, Jesus returned and I knew something was different. I wasn't sure what it was, but Andrew and I both noticed.

"Then one day Jesus came along while Andrew and I were helping our father clean the nets. He waved his usual greeting, the breeze from the sea whipping his hair and robe. He sat on the shore for a few minutes and watched us. Then he got up and motioned for us to follow him.[1]

"'Come follow me,' he said. 'Let's fish for people for awhile.'

"Andrew and I exchanged glances. We had expected this someday. Our father stopped his work and watched. He had known, also, the day would eventually come when we would leave. Andrew had already been following the Baptizer. We didn't know for sure what Jesus meant, but we knew the time had come. God's time was here. Jesus was ready to begin his new life, and Andrew and I wanted to be a part of it. We folded our nets and placed them in the boat. Our father fought back tears as he hugged us and gave us his blessing. We said farewell to him and followed Jesus on a new adventure."

Peter turned and walked back to the window. He hesitated, staring into the night. "It seems that I am always putting my foot in my mouth. I have a knack for saying the wrong thing, or somehow making the right words sound wrong."

"Really? We would never have guessed that." Snickers and giggles followed.

Peter, startled at the sound, turned so sharply he almost lost his balance. He put a hand out to catch himself against the wall. As he hastily looked from one to another, to discover who made the remark, he saw his brother, Andrew, grinning broadly at him. Lazarus was also grinning as he added in a tone of mock sincerity, "Yeah, Peter, who would ever have thought such a thing of you?"

Peter's haggard face reddened, and his dark eyes quickly narrowed and flashed darts of anger. Peter, a man of quick emotions, allowed the laughter which exploded all around to quickly soften his face into a smile. Anger drained from him. Shrugging his shoulders slightly and throwing his hands up in mock defeat, Peter grinned as he entered the jovial tone Lazarus and Andrew set. "I know," he said, "I'm normally such a cautious person!"

That was the breaking point. The whole room exploded into

laughter. Leah was wakened by the noise. "What's so funny?" she asked as she sat up and rubbed her eyes.

"Nothing," said Adam. "You were just dreaming about someone laughing." This brought more smothered laughter as they tried to let the little girl sleep, but she looked accusingly at her brother.

"The Commandments say, 'Thou shalt not lie,'" she said.[2]

Adam broke into more laughter. "I'm sorry," he said. "I'll tell you later. Right now, Peter is telling us his story."

"Oh. Well then, I'm going to stay awake and listen too," she declared, forcing her already round, inquisitive eyes more open than before.

Peter wiped his eyes from laughing so hard. Slowly he began to once again measure his words with his slow, even steps. "I know I have a way of saying the wrong thing, but Jesus always found it amusing – even as you do. He would just smile and say to me, 'Peter, you are indeed a rock. Someday, you will see how steady you are.'

"It was always fun to be with him – that is almost always. We did a lot of hard work – learning frustrating, coping kind of stuff. But we could laugh and have fun, too." He glanced at Lazarus and continued. "He would probably even find some humor in this night like you seem to do. You know – like all of us attempting to be serious and orthodox in our grieving, all the while tripping and falling over ourselves as we try to make sense of it all. He would have found a parable or riddle to tell us."

Peter struggled to gain a sense of hope such as Lazarus and some of the others seemed to have. Nevertheless, try as he would, he found himself falling into a sort of melancholy feeling again.

"We all lost a good friend and teacher," replied Lazarus, with compassion and understanding in his voice. "But the world hasn't ended yet, Peter. God is still in control. And somehow, I believe God will have the last Word, even as he had the first." Lazarus rose from his chair and moved to stand in front of Peter, looking him in the eye.

"I know in my heart you're right, Lazarus." Peter returned his friend's intent gaze. "Except sometimes my mind gets in the way of my heart." He dropped his gaze and turned to pace the opposite direction. Lazarus returned to his seat.

Agitation was again building within Peter, evaporating even the melancholy feeling. *If only I had room to really walk. I feel like I'm ready to explode!* His thoughts caused him to pound his fist so hard into his palm that he winced, shaking his hand to free the pain. Anger again was in control of his voice as he stood rubbing his hand. "I really believed Jesus was the Messiah. I thought he would declare himself King and end all oppression and pain. I gave up everything to follow him and waited patiently for that to happen. Well," his voice softened a little after his angry outburst, "maybe not patiently, but expectantly."

As quickly as his anger flared, it was extinguished. Once again he marveled at how emotions flip-flopped this night – not only his, but everyone's.

Peter smiled to himself. He glanced at John and shared his thought. "You talked earlier about the day we were on our way to Caesarea Philippi. If I remember correctly, that's when Jesus first told us he was going to Jerusalem. I didn't want to hear it. I couldn't understand why he would want to return to a place where the authorities had tried to stone him. Then I thought maybe this was it – you know – the time when he would set up his kingdom. How could he do anything if he got himself killed?"

Peter paused, took a couple of deep breaths and began once again. "I knew he hadn't forgotten, but I reminded him that there was a price on his head. I expected some off-hand remark, a story or a parable. He only smiled a sad kind of smile and said, 'I know.'"

The candles reflecting shadows on his wrinkled brow, and narrowed eyes gave Peter an ominous look. "He tried to explain how God reveals himself to us and has a plan our future, but I was pretty dense. Not until we went to Bethany and he brought Lazarus back from the grave did I even begin to halfway understand the wisdom and power of God. However, I can't help wondering, if he could bring back Lazarus back from the dead, why could he not have prevented his own death? How was it possible for the Son of

God, the Messiah, to suffer and die like he did?"

"We all were perplexed by those same questions, Peter." Andrew spoke as he watched his brother with a curious mixture of admiration and awe.

"I know," said Peter. "And yet somehow I thought I should have known better. After all, God had just revealed to me that Jesus was the Son of God. Couldn't God also have given me some insight into his death?"

Falling deeper and deeper into his self-pity, Peter rattled on, hardly noticing anything or anyone. "Surely, Jesus made a mistake in calling me. I should have stuck with fishing. I understand fish!"

He paused, took a few steps in his corner and began again. "Before I had a chance to talk to Jesus about my thoughts and feelings, things began to happen rapidly. Jesus said it was time to take his stand in Jerusalem. Of course, we thought that meant setting up his kingdom – overturning the Roman rule – giving Israel back its place of honor. So we got that little donkey for Jesus to ride into Jerusalem. We really wanted to put him on a white horse and have him ride in style, but he insisted on the donkey. He said it was a symbol of humility and servanthood. Jesus was obsessed with servanthood and humility. It made no sense to me. Jesus was the Messiah! I would have..." Peter's voice raised to a pitch of hot fervor and then dropped, trailing away for a moment. He paused, staring out the window at a faint hint of the approaching dawn.

Taking a deep breath, he turned and continued talking. "Oh, well," he sighed, shrugging his shoulders – a quickly developing habit that night. "We proceeded into the city amid the shouts of the people. As Adam told us, the children sang and waved palm branches. And you know, you're right," he said as he glanced at the youth. "Children do seem to grasp the situation much more quickly than we, who should know better. Jesus was honored that day by the children in a way we, his closest friends, would never have thought to do.

"It looked like we were on our way. Everything was working as it should. Within a few days we would have control of Jerusalem. Like a sudden gale on the sea, however, everything changed. It was not long until people began to murmur and complain, seeking his life."

"I will never understand how people can change their minds so quickly," said Martha with a note of anger and frustration. "They were so joyous and singing songs of triumph one day and hardly a week later they were yelling 'Crucify him.' How can people change their loyalty so quickly?"

"They didn't." This quiet remark from Nicodemus startled everyone. They almost forgot the little man from the Sanhedrin was there. Not really expecting an answer to the question, Martha was surprised by the sound of his voice. "What do you mean, Nicodemus?" she asked. "Of course they cried for his blood."

"But it wasn't the same crowd, Martha," he replied. "The first one was led by this young man, his friends, and the disciples. Their joy and excitement were contagious to others who had joined them. The second crowd – a mob really – was led by the rabble-rousers hired and planted by the chief priests and scribes. They were instructed to incite riots if necessary in order to get to Jesus and have him killed. That was a marvel in itself, since they wanted to get rid of Jesus in order to prevent a riot! There were no singing children or excited disciples in that second crowd – only men who wanted blood."

Martha's brow was knit in thought for a moment, her eyes fixed on Nicodemus. "That never occurred to me," she said. "You're probably right. Now that I think about it, we were all probably there the first time, and none of us were shouting with the second one." She paused to let the new idea soak into her thoughts. Then with a quick smile, she said, "Thank you, Nicodemus. That makes it a little easier to accept, knowing that at least it wasn't his friends who turned on him."

"We didn't turn on him," said Peter. His voice was full of anguish, his face contorted by grief. "But we turned away from him, which was just as bad." He paused, wiped his hand across his face, trying to erase the pain. "But that comes a little later in my story, I guess."

He took a gulp from his cup and a deep breath before proceeding. "Jesus brought us together for the Passover meal in the upper room of Mordecai's place. Mordecai had already prepared the Passover table for us – the bread, the cup, the plates of food to be passed. The prayers were recited as we entered the room. Although he still hadn't moved to set up his kingdom, we thought everything was perfect.

"Once again Jesus tried to teach us about servanthood and humility. He, who should have had the place of honor, began to act like a servant and wash our feet.[3] Well, of course, I would have none of that and I told him so. He said to me, 'Peter, if I don't wash your feet, you cannot really be a part of my life. It's important for me to do this.'

"So, true to form, I blurted out, 'then wash me all over – my head, my hands, my body.' Jesus smiled in spite of the seriousness of the occasion. I'm glad he could see beyond my foolishness and find humor and love." Peter smiled in spite of himself.

"'Peter,' he said, 'will you ever learn to think before speaking? This is only a symbol of cleansing for your daily walk. You've already been cleansed. Only your feet now need to be cleansed.' Needless to say, I felt rather foolish. I was glad that he loved and understood me. I vowed that I would learn to control my tongue."

"Did you?" asked Leah.

"Did I what?" returned Peter. He turned to face with confusion.

"Did you learn to control your tongue?"

Peter looked a little disconcerted at his brother. The other disciples snickered. "Well..." he started.

Before Peter could answer, Leah spoke again. "Never mind. I guess I shouldn't have asked that question. I just wondered if you did learn to control your tongue, how you did it. My brother is always telling me my tongue will get me in trouble."

Peter smiled at Leah, and for the first time felt a real kinship to this outrageously honest little girl. Maybe Jesus had the right attitude about children after all! "No, Leah, I haven't learned yet. I'm still working on it," he said. Then he continued his story.

"We were nearing the end of the meal when Jesus began talking about being betrayed and deserted." He flashed a quick smile at Leah. "Only minutes after vowing to think first, talk later, I lost the battle.

I had to know what he was talking about. I couldn't understand what he meant by being betrayed. What was he doing that everyone didn't already know? He openly proclaimed his message. I thought it might have had something to do with the earlier attempt on his life, but surely if the Sanhedrin wanted him they knew where he was at any time of the day."

"Not really, Peter." Nicodemus' words startled him. Peter turned to face the little man from the Sanhedrin who had already added so much to their night of memories. "Many members of the Sanhedrin never heard Jesus themselves. They only knew about him through others. It would've been impossible to arrest him while he was preaching without causing a riot – and that's what they were, in their own warped way, trying to prevent. They didn't know where to find him at other times of the day or night where he wouldn't be protected by crowds of followers. So they looked and listened for anyone willing to lead them to him."

Peter was glad to have someone give even a little bit of understanding in this senseless time of his life. "Jesus knew someone would tell them where he would be, but I still didn't know what he was talking about. I had to know, so I got John's attention and asked him to find out what Jesus meant. Who was going to betray him, and how? He must be talking about one of the many followers outside our little group of twelve. I was sure none of us would ever betray Jesus. I could feel the anger boiling within me. I was ready to go find the betrayer and take care of him!"

Once again, interrupted by the child's voice, Peter turned to face Leah. "Why did you ask John to find out?" she questioned. "Why didn't you ask Jesus yourself? Were you afraid he would call you Satan again?"

Peter's brow knit together and he pulled at his beard deep in thought. "I'm not really sure, Leah." Peter was quiet for a minute, pressing his fingers into his temples. It was not his nature to think. He was an action person. Finally, the words began to flow again, haltingly at first. "No...I wasn't afraid of him...I was never afraid of him...full of awe maybe...but not fear. I guess I thought he might be giving us one of his riddles or a parable or something. It didn't seem possible that anyone would really betray him. I guess I thought John would know how, and what, to ask."

"John was sitting closer to Jesus at the time," interjected Andrew. "The rest of us wondered also, but we didn't want to ask. We were glad you asked John to speak for us." Andrew smiled at this brother.

Peter frowned. "It seems the rest of you were willing, on more than one occasion, to let me put my foot in my mouth, while you benefited without getting into trouble."

Andrew laughed. "Well, no use all of us stumbling like an idiot when you were so willing to do it for us."

"Thanks a lot," said Peter sarcastically. He felt more tension and pain as he remembered that night which he would rather forget. He knew if he lived to be a hundred he would never forget it.

"Jesus told John the betrayer was the one to whom he would give the bite of bread, and then he handed a piece to Judas. When I heard that, I felt more than a little shaken. Did he really mean Judas would betray him? Why didn't Judas deny it? Surely he understood the intent of Jesus' words. Judas was a trusted friend, a disciple. He was one of us. We even trusted him with our money – not that there was a lot of it. We couldn't just turn on him without proof, and yet, did we dare mistrust Jesus' words?"

The words continued to tumble out of Peter's mouth like a stream of water fed by a sudden downpour. "I thought maybe I had misunderstood – again. I felt frustrated. If Jesus had said it was someone outside our intimate circle of friends who would betray him, I wouldn't have given it another thought. I would have jumped immediately and taken care of him. It would have been easy to fight someone I didn't know personally. But how could I quarrel with Judas? What if I were wrong? Then they all would be angry with me – even Jesus."

His words halted. Slowly turning to face his friends, he smiled toward Leah, a strange look on his face. "Can you believe it? I was actually thinking before I spoke. The one time when I should have spoken first and thought later, and I took time to think about it!"

Leah understood. She placed her hands over her mouth and giggled as Peter continued. "Before I could decide what to do about it, Judas left and Jesus began talking about the all the rest of us falling away. It was such an incredible thing for him to say that I immediately forgot Judas. How could he even think such a thing? I told him I didn't know about the rest of them, but I would certainly never abandon him, even if I had to die with him. And I really meant it." His voice faded. "I thought I was strong."

All his life Peter had prided himself on his strength. He was not accustomed to being soft and shedding so many tears. Recent events had so turned his whole world upside-down, he couldn't think clearly. He never knew what feelings would erupt next.

Choking back a sob that tried to escape from his throat, Peter turned toward the window. "Jesus asked a strange question in light of what I had just declared. He asked if I would really die for him, then gazing directly into my eyes, as if he could see the future written there, he answered his own question. 'Yes, Peter, you will indeed give up your life for me. Not tonight, nor very soon. However, before the dawn comes tomorrow, before the cock crows in the morning, you will deny even knowing me three times.'"[5]

Peter's words were almost lost as he bowed his head, his shoulders slumped. Lifting his head slightly, he turned back to face his friends. His face was gaunt and gray. "I was shocked. Surely Jesus didn't say what I thought I heard him say. How can he even think such a thing? I knew I would never deny him and turn away."

There was a long pause and Peter tried to make his inner feelings match the mask of self-confidence his outer shell displayed. "And yet..." He struggled to keep his voice from trembling. "...And yet, when that cock crowed the following morning, his words burned into my soul like the coal on Isaiah's lips."

Peter sighed deeply, glanced at the ceiling and back to his friends. "In the garden where Jesus went to pray, he needed my friendship and I slept. When the mob tried to take him captive, I drew my sword and swung it furiously, not even caring who felt its blade, forgetting how Jesus felt about violence. I was as surprised as the servant of the high priest when his ear fell to the ground. I was even more surprised and bewildered when Jesus quietly bent and picked up the ear and replaced it on the man's head. The bleeding stopped immediately. The pain had not yet even registered." Peter placed a hand over an ear, feeling the pain the servant never felt.

"He hardly looked at me while he healed that man, but then he turned and spoke to me. His voice sounded sharp, but his eyes spoke love. 'Don't use the sword. We don't want violence.' And then he was gone. They took him away. While I watched helplessly, they bound him and led him down the path. I heard him say, 'Leave them alone. I'm the one you want.' I knew they wanted the rest of us, too. We all fled, fearing for our own lives! I had to know where they were taking him, so I followed far enough behind that none would know I belonged to his disciples. I tried to rationalize my actions, thinking, how could I help him if they captured me? If they didn't know I was one of his disciples, maybe I could get inside and help him escape."

Peter shuddered as the chill wind of memory blew over him. "I did deny him three times. I even cursed when asked if I knew him." He looked helplessly from one to another. Seeing an empty chair near Andrew, he dropped onto it. All energy suddenly drained from him, and his legs would no longer hold him upright. Dropping his head in his hands, he sat very still. The hush and quiet in the room were almost unbearable. Andrew raised himself half out of his chair, preparing to help his brother, but Peter began talking again and Andrew eased himself back onto his chair.

"How could I have done such things?" he asked quietly – not really expecting an answer from anyone. "Instantly, I thought I knew how Judas must have felt. He must have thought his betrayal would force Jesus to make his move. I never saw such a look of agony as was on his face when the Temple Police took Jesus away that night. He tried to stop them when he realized Jesus would do nothing to prevent his capture. The officers pushed him aside like he was a stray mongrel. Remembering Judas, my own betrayal seemed far more unacceptable. I wept until I thought I had no more tears left.

165

But I've found there were, and are, still more to come."

Peter sat quietly, his hands folded in his lap, his head bowed. "I remembered how Jesus said I would deny him, and I knew I had to find Judas. I wasn't sure why, but I knew I had to find him. I ran from the courtyard, stumbling and tripping over twigs and stones. A week ago I would have said I didn't know how to cry – nor did I need to know. Now the tears keep returning. They blinded me as I ran in search of Judas.

"The burning love in Jesus' eyes followed me, haunting me. Someone grabbed my cloak and tried to stop me. Leaving him holding a torn piece from my sleeve, I ran on, not knowing where I was going, nor even caring. I only knew I had to find Judas. I had to know if he shared my grief and my guilt – and I, his. I had to know what possessed him – and me – to betray our Lord. Neither of us deserved to live. When I found Judas, I thought maybe I would kill him, and then myself."

A gasp or two was heard at such a comment. Peter ignored it, lost in his memories. He continued. "I ran through the streets, knocking over a cart here and there, tripping over a dog scrounging for a bite to eat. The women were on their way to the well. At least I had presence of mind enough to swerve so as not to run them over.

"The sun moved higher in the sky, shining more brightly than it had a right to, promising a new day of gladness when there was none. Birds sang in the trees as if it was a normal day.

"Trying to block out the sights and sounds, I stumbled on. I was headed for the Potter's Field, although I had no idea I chose that destination – if I chose it. I just wanted to escape those burning, loving, sad eyes of Jesus who had trusted me. Oh, yes, I betrayed Jesus just as surely as Judas did. I betrayed him." Peter's voice cracked. His eyes filled with fresh tears. Andrew rose, but Peter waved him back. He had to finish – pain or not.

Brushing aside the tears, sighing deeply again, he pressed on. He had no choice now. The words flowed like water over a broken dam. "Finally, breathless, I reached the field of broken pots and stones. Here and there an olive tree or fig tree tried gallantly to grow out of the rubble. I went to the edge of a deep crevice, thinking I would throw myself over the edge to the rocks below. I could not live with my guilt.

"I was about to hurl myself over the edge when a sound behind me caught my attention. It...it... sounded like...like the soft crying of a very young child, or even an infant. I could not imagine who would or could leave a child out in such a desolate place. When I turned, I caught sight of a movement in a small cluster of briars.

"The crevice called to me. I could almost hear from the depths of it, 'Come on down, Peter. You don't deserve to live.' From behind me, the soft crying continued and the movement in the brush increased. If a child was lost in there... Well, my troubles could wait. I just had to go see.

"I pulled at the twigs, branches and wild, matted briars. They came out, roots and all. There was no child, but a lamb was caught in the brambles – a little white lamb! I was so distraught at the time it didn't occur to me to wonder where it came from. I have since had many questions: Why was a lamb in that God-forsaken place? Where was its mother? Where was the shepherd? Why didn't I hear it when I first arrived? I couldn't understand, but I knew somehow God provided a lamb for my salvation! No longer did I feel the need to kill Judas or end my own life. I felt only the need to weep. I sat there holding the lamb and weeping bitterly until a cry from the crevice on the other side of the boulders caught my attention.

"I ran to see who or what it was, but I was too late. Hanging from a straggly olive tree, which could hardly bear its own weight, was Judas. He was dead. And I wept for him as I had wept for myself. While I stood there helpless, weeping like a child, the poor little tree began to lean toward the crevice. It was no longer able to hold the weight of Judas. The grief and guilt which drove him to destruction was too much for even that little tree to bear. Still hanging from its branches, Judas and the tree fell to the stony ground below. I felt numb."

An awe-filled, almost reverent hush fell over the room. Peter sat quietly for so long, they wondered if he had finished his story. No one could find a voice to speak. Finally, with great effort, Peter turned to face Adam. He uttered the words almost mechanically, "When I saw Judas, something died within me. I don't think we ever get around those changes which forever remove some part of life as we knew it. It's a type of death.

"New waves of sadness washed over me as I saw Judas' body settle on the stones below. The carefree days of Jesus and the twelve of us together were gone forever. One lay dead in Potter's Field and Jesus, himself, was in grave danger. Could I yet do something? I didn't know.

"At least I could take the little lamb that had saved my life and care for it. However, when I turned to get it, it was gone. Somehow I knew it was useless to search, but I tried anyway. I looked everywhere. It simply was not there. I knew then I was called back from the brink of death by an angel of God. I left that place of death and returned to Jerusalem hoping to see Jesus and ask his forgiveness.

"By the time I returned, the crowd had moved to Golgotha. I followed. There was nothing more I could do for Jesus, as there had been nothing more I could do for Judas. The die was cast. Before the day ended, Jesus and Judas would meet again, and Jesus would have the last word."

Peter stopped, feeling as exhausted as he had when he returned from Potter's Field. Memories clung furiously and would not be washed away by his tears. He sat motionless, staring out into the graying darkness, not wanting to face the others yet.

Finally, gaining a few remaining threads of courage, he faced his friends and began weaving in the ends of the story. "Yes, Adam, I was there. I stood off in a distance hiding behind the brush and clinging to a little olive tree much like the one I had seen Judas on. I didn't deserve to be near him. I couldn't bear for him to see me, or for me to look into those sad, loving eyes. It wasn't easy to remember all those flippant, joyous times when we had joked and shared riddles. How much I longed to just once again hear him say, 'Look, Pete, you know I love you.' When I came here, I didn't think I could ever laugh again, but this night has taught me sometimes tears and laughter cannot be separated."

Making a sweeping motion with his arm, Peter gave credit to all his friends for his renewing sense of hope. "You have all given me joy in remembering and a sense of hope for joy to come."

Peter sighed heavily as he glanced once more at the window – looking for the dawn, hoping it would delay its arrival. "Soon it will be dawn. Is it be possible you are right, Lazarus? Is there still hope?"

Not expecting nor waiting for a reply, Peter again dropped his head in his hands. He was tired. He would just simply wait for the dawn. In the distance somewhere he heard the first crow of a rooster telling the world dawn was on its way. This time it was not in his memory. It was real. Maybe...just maybe...

The tears flowed freely again. Peter thought no one could ever have confidence in him again after his confession of betrayal. Surprised by light touch to his arm, he raised his head to look into the wide, dark eyes of Leah.

"Mr. Peter," she declared, "Jesus loves you." And she placed her arms around his neck. Peter folded her in his arms, and together they wept for their loss. Then she giggled as only a child can giggle. "Your beard tickles my face just like Jesus' beard did," she laughed. Together they laughed through their tears.

Chapter Twelve

And Mary Pondered...

Peter's tears continued to flow intermittently as feelings of remorse and hope were woven together – remorse for what he had done and not done, and hope that Lazarus might be right. Mesmerized by his own thoughts, he almost forgot the child on his lap.

Mary, Jesus' mother, stood, stretched her arms, and slowly moved around the room. Stopping beside Peter, she laid her hand on his shoulder. "You were always a faithful friend, Simon Peter." She had called him by both names from the time he and Jesus were very young. "No one could have prevented his death. I guess I knew that all along, but never wanted to think about it. He loved you, Simon Peter, and understood you even better than you understand yourself. Whatever he had in mind as far as a kingdom, you will be included – whatever and wherever that will be."

Lovingly Mary caressed the child's soft hair. "Jesus used to have hair this soft when he was little like you," she murmured. A quick, sad smile spread across her face. "His was more of a chestnut brown. He never wanted to have it cut."

Mary sighed and moved back to her chair by the window where she could continue her vigil for the coming dawn. The others turned to watch with her. They wanted to comfort her, but didn't know what to say or do.

"Tell us about Jesus," said Leah. "When he was little like me, I mean."

"Leah, maybe she would rather not talk about that now," said Miriam, who moved to take her daughter back to sit with her.

"Oh, it's all right." Mary turned to Miriam with a smile. "It's been comforting to be with friends who aren't afraid to share their memories. The night hasn't seemed so long. Death is painful for those of us who survive, but it has eased my pain to hear your joyous memories of my son. You've all been good to share them with me. Maybe it will ease my pain more to share some of my own memories."

Turning to Leah, Mary smiled. "Would you like to come and sit with me for a while? It's been a long time since I held a little girl on my lap."

Leah glanced at Peter, who nodded to her. She jumped down and ran to Mary. Making herself comfortable on Mary's lap, Leah watched her intently. If nothing else, the curious, questioning little girl was learning patience from the night of vigil.

Mary took her time thinking and pondering where to begin. Finally, deciding on a course of direction, she began. "My life with Jesus really began long before he was born. Even as a child I was being prepared and didn't know it. While it was a long time ago, it seems only yesterday that I was a young girl at home waiting for my betrothed to come and take me to his home. I had been promised to Joseph, the carpenter from Nazareth, from the time I was about eight. Our families knew each other a long time. Joseph was older than I, but he was content to wait until I was old enough to become his bride. When the time came, we began planning for the wedding feast. Unusual things started happening, beginning with a visit from an angel."[1]

Mary was very quiet for a few moments, not sure how much she really wanted to share. She decided the others needed to know as much as possible to settle grief and have memories to pass on. "Sometimes, when I close my eyes, I can see that angel just as clearly as if it was yesterday. He said, 'You are going to have a son and you will name him Jesus.'"

"You really saw an angel?" asked Leah. Her dark eyes opened even wider. "What did he look like? Did he have wings?"

Mary laughed and hugged Leah close to her. It was easy to regain her own childish delight with someone like Leah to keep reminding her. "I don't remember wings. However, I was so frightened, I'm not sure now how much of what I remember is real, and how much is what I think I remember. One thing I know for sure, he was a messenger from God. There was a sort of glow about him that made him different." Mary paused, trying to recall the image of that messenger who had turned her world upside-down. With a dreamy look in her eyes, she continued her thought. "Except for the white robe, the angel looked pretty much like any other person of modest means."

Leah clapped her hands together in delight. "A real angel? Where were you? Were you at home? Did the angel come to your house?"

"There was a hill near our home. About half-way up was a small clearing, partially hidden by low bushes on two sides, and the rock wall of the mountain on the back side. Inside the small opening, I had built my own altar to God. My mother taught me the stories of our Scriptures from the time I was toddling around her skirts. I especially liked the stories of Ruth and Esther and of our ancestors. Sometimes I would pretend that I was Ruth or Miriam or Sarah. My imagination kept me company."

Mary smiled as she thought about those happy days of childhood when she could be anyone she wanted to be. "That's where the angel visited me. Because I had spent so much time there in my imagination, I wasn't sure the angel was real."

Mary paused, a look of contentment on her face. "I loved just being with God there. My heart could be pounding with fear and childish anxiety, and God would comfort me. My life would be overflowing with joy, and I'm sure I heard God laugh with me." She paused, then continued wistfully. "Sometimes...sometimes I wish I could go back to that quieter, simpler time of life."

Peter shifted in his chair and sipped the hot drink someone placed in his hand. As long as he had known Jesus and his family, he never heard Mary talk about her life. She told them of the stable in Bethlehem, but usually she was quiet and thoughtful, like she had been most of the night. He brought his attention back to her words.

"As the day of my marriage drew nearer, I was anxious about my future as a wife and eventually a mother. I needed to think, so I sought solitude in that special place and waited for God's calming presence to assure me everything would be all right. God had always quieted my heart and blessed me, but that day I received a blessing filled with wonder and awe – and even fear – such as I never knew before. I guess I was like you, Leah," she said as she looked down at the child on her lap. "Later the thought hit me, I saw a real angel! After the angel left, I sat for a little while, just trying to understand. Then I knew, whatever else I did, I had to find my mother and tell her what the angel said. She would know what to do."

"What did your mother say?" asked Leah.

Mary thought for a minute then continued. "Well, I ran until our house was in sight. It wasn't far." Mary smiled at her, stroking the child's soft hair. "By the time I reached the door, the day had suddenly gone and dusk was upon us. I was gone longer than I intended. A candle was already being lit as I hurried inside. My mind was churning with questions running through my mind. *What will Mother and Father say or do when I tell them the angel's message? Will they disown me? Will Joseph refuse to follow through with our marriage plans?*

"My father asked 'Where have you been? Your mother needed you to...' and his words fell unspoken as he faced me. My mother, also, turned and immediately ran to me.

"'Mary! What is it? What is wrong?' she asked. 'You look like you have seen a ghost. You look...' Her words, also, fell silent.

"I had to say something. I decided a straight-forward, matter-of-fact approach would be best. 'Not a ghost, Mother,' I answered much more calmly than I felt. 'I saw an angel.' I was actually feeling the calm and quiet by the time I finished speaking. God was with me.

"'I saw an angel,' I repeated with a little more courage, 'and I have news – no, I have an announcement for you.' I swallowed, trying hard to keep the tears from falling down my face. 'I'm going to have a baby.' Then my voice just quit. No more words would come out of my mouth.

"Both my parents spoke as one. 'You what?' They stood staring at me as if I had spoken an unknown language. Color drained from their faces."

Mary laughed. The sound was like a bubbling water fall. "It's funny now as I remember the expression on their faces, but it wasn't funny then. Both my parents turned ashen. I hurried with my news, trying to be quick and to the point for them.

"'The angel told me that for some reason I have found favor in God's eyes and I will bear God's Son. His name will be Jesus.' There, it was out. It all sounded so simple, but the color drained even more from my mother's face, if that could be possible. I was afraid she might faint.

"'Mary!' she exclaimed. 'That's not something to joke about. It's blasphemous!'

"'I'm not joking, Mother,' I answered. 'I'm very serious.' I could hold back the tears no longer – tears of joy, of fear, of nervous tension. 'Oh, Mother, Father, what am I to do? How will I tell Joseph?'

"A strange feeling of loneliness and fear suddenly surrounded me so heavily I felt I was smothering. The child that I was, despite my age, could stand it no longer. I flung myself into their arms and we clung together until the tears stopped flowing.

"When I was calm again, my parents sat down with me and spoke almost as one, 'Start at the beginning and tell us again what happened. Don't leave anything out.' And then my mother added, her face twisted almost into a question mark, 'An angel?' It would have been funny if it wasn't so serious."

"God likes to do that," stated Leah, as if she were an expert.

"Do what, Leah?" asked Mary, feeling her own face form into a question mark.

"Oh, you know. When something is supposed to be one way, God likes to switch it just so we don't get so...so...know-it-all."

A few seconds of dead silence was followed by an explosion of laughter.

"Well, he does," maintained Leah, falling into a pout.

Mary hugged her close. "We aren't laughing at you, dear," she said, still laughing. "We are laughing at ourselves because we know you're right. We set rules and expect God to abide by them, forgetting God is the maker of all rules. We say angels don't visit people. God says, 'Why not?' Thank you, Leah, for your insight."

Leah wasn't sure she understood all Mary said, but she felt loved and praised, and she beamed with pleasure.

Glancing toward Joshua, Mary wiped the remaining tears of laughter from her face and smiled. "I think I felt a little like you did when the Priests and Pharisees kept asking you to repeat your story of how you gained your sight. I guess some news is just so difficult to believe it must be repeated over and over." She then turned her attention back to the child on her lap, giving her another little hug.

"So, I started at the beginning and told them everything again – the angel, the message, the feelings. They were as concerned as I was about what Joseph would think and do.

"'Can this be true?' My mother looked to my father for help in understanding. 'Mary has never lied to us before, but she has such an active imagination. If it's true, what will we tell Joseph? What can we tell him? We've already paid the dowry. She's married to him in all but the formal celebration. And...'

"Her voice died away as we all realized there could be no celebration. The anguish in my father's eyes reminded us of the penalty of adultery – for who would believe such an announcement? It was difficult even for my parents, who knew and loved me. Who could believe that a child, who had suddenly become a woman, was about to become the mother of the Son of the Most High? Even though every Jewish girl from the time of the prophets hoped to be the chosen one, no one really believed it would happen. And especially like this! She would be some bride of a prince in a palace, maybe, but surely not to an unmarried, poor girl." Even yet, awe filled her voice as Mary told her story.

Pausing long enough to glance out the window, she saw the sky was still dark with a hint of light somewhere off in the distance, east of Jerusalem. An unexplained tension was building around the room. Time was moving quickly. Whatever the new day would hold, this was a night for memories which would see them through the rest of their days.

Mary went on with her story. "I remembered one more bit of the news the angel gave me. What could be more devastating than to hear your daughter is with child before consummating the marriage – and not even the groom's child? You are certainly right, Leah. It seems every time God sends a heavenly messenger, someone's life gets turned upside-down.

"The second bit of news I gave them was as hard to believe as the first. The angel told me my cousins, Elizabeth and Zechariah, were also going to be parents.[2] My parents were stunned. My mother finally found her voice. 'Elizabeth? And Zechariah? You must be mistaken. They are...they have to be eighty-something.' I had never seen my mother so speechless.

"I told her I thought so, too, but the angel must have already read my thoughts. Before I could say anything to him, he told me that nothing is impossible with God."

"Then what did you do? I bet your mother knew what you should do next." Leah's eyes sparkled.

Mary chuckled, a soft rippling sound that warmed the grieving hearts. The acute grief and frustration of earlier hours was lifting like the mist of a summer's morn. Was it the memories or the child's influence? Or was God getting ready to turn the world upside-down...again?

"Yes, Leah," Mary answered. "My mother was a jewel who knew what to do most of the time. She said we would all leave early the next morning and visit Elizabeth. If indeed she was pregnant, then I would stay for a while with her. We would tell Joseph the truth and let God take care of the results. My great announcement had surely turned our world upside-down, but we wondered what it would do to the rest of world. A Messiah born to a poor girl of Nazareth? It was beyond belief. Mother did believe – sort of – but she needed to hear it from Elizabeth.

"By the time we returned from our visit with Elizabeth, my body had begun to make the changes of pregnancy. While I was not very large yet, it was evident I was different. I wondered how I could face

Joseph and my friends. Telling him was probably the most difficult thing I have ever done – except possibly standing by that cross the other day." Her voice dropped to almost a whisper on the final words.

She took a moment to collect the rest of her thoughts and then continued to speak in a clear voice once again, loud enough for all to hear. "But even though Joseph didn't understand, he was kind to me. Others did not really matter as long as Joseph continued to love me. And he did, even when people smiled and nodded their heads and whispered behind our backs.

"Oh, at first he thought briefly about divorcing me quietly, so that I would not be put to shame or to death. An angel came to him in a dream and told him it was all right to take me as his wife.[3] Joseph was a godly man and he obeyed without question."

"Another angel!" exclaimed Leah. "I wish I could see a real angel."

"You've seen someone much greater than an angel, dear child. You've seen Jesus." Mary understood Leah's desire to have a special message from God.

"Oh," said Leah, brightening, the pout disappearing. "That's right. I don't need to see an angel because Jesus held me and blessed me. I'm his child, too!"

"You certainly are, my dear," said Mary as she smiled at the little girl.

"Tell me about when Jesus was born," pleaded Leah. "Adam says he was born in a stable. Is that true?"

"Yes, it's true. As the time drew near for my son to be born, I became a little fearful and anxious. And then came the tax. Caesar, for some reason which I have never understood, needed a head tax. Possibly he was fulfilling God's promise of long ago without even realizing it. Whatever the reason, everyone had to go to the home of their ancestors to be counted and taxed.

"Joseph wanted me to stay in Nazareth, but I was too frightened to stay alone. I wasn't afraid of people or animals, and I knew my mother would come if I needed her, but I was afraid Joseph wouldn't be with me when the baby was born. And that was very important to me, even though most of my friends laughed at me. They couldn't understand why I would want a man around at a time like that. But I did. I wanted Joseph to be with me.

"So we made the long trip to Bethlehem. I rode the little donkey most of the way. It took us several days. When we got there, dusk was falling. They almost didn't let us in the city gates. After a frantic search for a place to sleep for the night, we were given a stall in a stable behind the Bethlehem Inn. I knew my time was drawing near, but I really thought we would be able to pay our tax and return to Nazareth in time. I didn't expect to give birth in Bethlehem. And in a stable yet! However, it was warm and sheltered from the night winds. Joseph was with me, and as a big, beautiful star sent its light like a torch through the tiny window, Jesus was born.[4]

"Not long after the birth, excited shepherds came. They told us about angels singing to them and telling them where to find the baby.[5] Much later we were visited by kings who brought strange gifts – gold, frankincense and myrrh.[6] At least they seemed strange to us at the time. I thought of those kings as I stood by the cross and I wondered what they would think if they were here today."

"They probably would go get their armies and come back and kill all the bad guys," said Leah with all the fury of a child trying to be an adult.

Mary laughed in spite of the seriousness. Leah's fury caught her off-guard. "You may be right, Leah. However, I don't think Jesus would approve."

Leah looked surprised, and then repentant. "No, I guess I really don't think so either." Then she changed the subject, eager to hear about Jesus when he was young like her. "Was Jesus a good baby?" she asked.

Mary smiled again at the way Leah's mind could jump from one topic to another without losing a beat. "Oh, yes. He hardly ever cried. He did cry, of course. All babies do. They have to if they are healthy. But he didn't cry excessively. When he learned to smile, his whole face beamed. He was such a bundle of joy to hold in my arms.

"Everything seemed to be going well for us, and then we learned King Herod was angry with the kings from the East. They didn't go back and tell him where my baby was, as he had ordered them to do. An angel again appeared to Joseph and warned him to take us to Egypt immediately. We left in the pre-dawn hours with hardly enough light to see the path before us, just missing an awful massacre of little children."[7] Mary shuddered at the remembered slaughter.

"I remember that night," said Joshua's mother. "It was selfish of me, but I gave thanks to Yahweh that my blind baby was too old to be killed. It was awful. We lived in Bethlehem a short time. After that awful time, we felt it would be better to return to the region of Galilee."

Joshua laid his arm on his mother's shoulder as if he could protect her from fears of the past. She had been through so much because of him. Now it was his turn to return what help and love he could.

Mary nodded. "I don't think it was selfish at all. I'm sure there were many thankful mothers, as well as many grieving ones for many months. We stayed in Egypt until we knew Herod was dead. An angel once again told us it was safe to return to Nazareth, where we settled down. Joseph opened his carpenter's shop and I began my work as a homemaker.[8]

"Jesus grew and played with the other children of the village, climbing trees, roaming the hills, even fishing once in a while. He helped Joseph in the shop and learned the trade. We hoped he would eventually find a nice girl and settle down, but deep in my heart I knew that would not be possible. Always resounding somewhere in the back of my mind were his words when we found him in the temple the day Lazarus told you about. He said, 'Didn't you know I had to learn about my Father's business?'

"As he grew older, he seemed to lose interest in the carpenter shop. He preferred being with people, listening to them. Over and over they told him their stories – many times repeating them. He listened as if it was the first time he heard them. And the children of the village loved to come to him and listen to the stories he could tell."

Leah looked into Mary's eyes and smiled nodding her head in agreement. "He really could tell good stories. And he didn't care if we interrupted him to ask something," she said.

Mary smiled and continued. "Sometimes he would make the children laugh and sometimes he would be more serious, giving riddles for them to solve. It always delighted him when they could solve his riddles. He would say to me, 'The children know more about the Kingdom of God than most adults.' It puzzled me when he spoke with such passion. I added those times to the already numerous thoughts I kept in my heart." Mary paused, searching her memories for the next story.

"I remember well that day John was baptizing in the River Jordan and Jesus said he was going to be baptized. When I asked him why, he said it was necessary in God's plan of salvation. I was more bewildered. I wanted to know what was happening in my son's life, so I went along to watch.

"I couldn't wait until we got home and I could ask Jesus about the voice we heard," continued Mary. "However, when he left the river, he turned toward the wilderness. I ran after him and asked when he would be back. He said there were many things that he had to think about. I knew then our lives would never be the same. He gave me a kiss and turned away with that look of determination on his face I knew so well. There would be no stopping him. Lazarus followed. As he said, he was also turned back.

"His brothers and sisters and I were at the wedding of some friends in Cana when he returned. The groom's mother, Rachel, and I were close friends. We grew up together in Nazareth. It was a beautiful wedding. Unfortunately, more friends came than were expected. They were people of modest means and her husband, Jacob, hadn't been able to save enough wine for the occasion. He was a hard worker and such a good man. I didn't want him and Rachel to be shamed in the eyes of the village, so when Jesus arrived, I was overjoyed. I knew he would be able to think of something, so I asked him to help.

"I'm not sure what I expected him to do. I just knew that, even when he was a child, if I really needed help, he would come up with a solution. He had a sharp mind and could see what others would often miss. I knew he wouldn't let our friends suffer shame. Even so, I wasn't prepared for the kind of miracle he gave us. Water to wine! The servants filled the water pots with water and dipped out wine. I couldn't believe it![9]

"I asked Jesus how he did that. He just laughed the way he used to when he was a boy and said, 'Mother, you asked me to help, didn't you? Accept God's gifts and don't worry about how it's done.'"

James laughed. "You think you were surprised, you should have seen the look on the faces of those servants." James laughed again. "Jesus told them to fill the water pots which were used for ceremonial hand-washing with water. They obeyed, thinking the party would be over soon with no more wine available. Maybe the guests would need to have water poured over their hands before leaving."

"You should have seen their look when Jesus told them to take a dipper full to the chief steward for tasting." Andrew was laughing so hard he could say no more, so Thomas picked up the story.

"You call me a doubter! They were really caught between a rock and a hard place. Jesus told them to go and Mary told them to listen to him, but if they took water to the chief steward, he would have their heads."

"They finally shrugged and took the dipper to the steward," said John. "They were really shocked when he declared it the best wine he had ever tasted."

"Talk about being scared," added Nathaniel, also still chuckling, "they didn't know what to think. They knew they had taken water, not wine, to the steward. I saw them sip it as they returned for more. When they saw Jesus smiling at them, they backed away like they had seen a ghost."

"It was one of those fun times," said Peter, smiling.

Mary laughed so hard it brought tears. She paused, wiping her eyes, and glanced out the window for signs of the fast approaching dawn. Then she proceeded, feeling an urgency to finish before dawn shattered their night together.

"After the wedding, it seemed that Jesus began to drift away from us. Of his many friends he chose twelve to be with him all the time. I thought he was in no danger. He could take care of himself. Back home in Nazareth, though, we began to hear rumors of how he was behaving strangely. Some were even saying he must be possessed by demons. We were worried, so his brothers and I tried to get him to come home for a rest. Knowing how absorbed in his work he could be, we thought maybe he was working too hard. He loved people and could easily forget to even eat and sleep if someone needed him.

"We found the house where he was teaching. It was so crowded we couldn't get in. I was very proud of my son, all those people flocking to hear him. And yet, my pride was overshadowed by fear – almost as if I could see a darkness creeping in around the house. I tried to shake it off as we sent word to him that we were there.[10]

"His answer caused more concern. 'My mother and brothers? Who are they? Everyone who follows my Father is my mother and brothers,' he said. His brothers became quite upset. How could he do that to us – to me? Even through my sense of mixed pride and fear, I began to understand. I thought his answer must be one of his riddles he loved so much. The fear remained, but I relaxed, thinking he meant only to say he was all right and all people were as important to him as we were. Jesus wanted everyone to love God as much as I loved my son. Only by doing the will of the Father could anyone love that much.

"So I told his brothers we must return to Nazareth and leave Jesus alone. He knew what he was doing and God was with him. My sons didn't understand, but they knew better than to argue with their mother." Mary smiled and winked at Leah, who giggled.

"I know better than to argue with my mother," she said, holding her hand over her mouth to hide her giggles.

"Sure you do," said Adam sarcastically.

Mary laughed. "Sometimes you just know when you can and when you can't get away with something. That day they knew they couldn't. On our way back to Nazareth with my limited knowledge, I tried to explain to them who Jesus was and why he was doing what he was doing. They tried to be understanding, but it was hard for them, especially when people in the village laughed and called their brother crazy. They couldn't say, 'Our mother says he acts that way because he's the Son of God.' The village would soon think we were all crazy!

"We tried to keep up with where he was and what he was doing. We learned of people who were healed and made whole, and of lives that were changed because of him. It was impossible to hear it all. This night has been wonderful for me. It has filled in some of stories I knew only as outlines.

"Then, just about a week ago when he rode into Jerusalem, I was so proud of him, even if he did ride a donkey! I couldn't believe all those people who lined the streets and shouted 'Hosanna! Hosanna!' And you children with palm branches and songs of honor and respect. I guess we all were hoping that he would to set up his kingdom and make everything right for our people."

Mary paused. A lone tear trickled down her cheek. Before she could brush it away, she felt small fingers on her face. Smiling and hugging the child close to her, she continued. "All has changed now. I can understand how his words would anger the authorities, but I don't understand how they could call him a criminal and crucify him like that. We all know how loving and forgiving he was, but it's still hard to understand how he could have been so quiet and forgiving while hanging there on that cross.[11] And truly they didn't know what they were doing. They couldn't know they were crucifying their only means of redemption, and yet, how often he had tried to tell them."

Mary smiled and turned to John. "Jesus knew how much I loved him. He knew how difficult it was for me to stand there and watch him slowly dying on that cross." Her voice cracked as she remembered the scene. She paused, taking a deep breath.

"I would have given everything I own if they had put me there in his place. And he knew that. I thought my heart would truly break when he looked at me and used his precious breath to comfort me. 'Woman, see your son,' he said.[12] It was so little and yet so much. Knowing him so well, I knew he meant, 'Mother, I love you. I can no longer be the son you need to take care of you and love you.' And his words to John, 'See your mother,' meant the same."[13]

Mary paused as if in deep thought. She was reliving all those beautiful and horrible memories. When she spoke again, her voice was a little husky. "You have all been so kind. Simon Peter," she turned to face him, "you said you felt you should have known better because God had given you a special revelation. Well, I guess I felt I should be able to understand, too. After all, I am his mother! And God..." She left the thought hanging in the air.

"Jesus said he was the Messiah. He said he would be raised in three days. But...I don't understand. He shouldn't have died in the first place. He should not have died..." Her voice became gradually softer.

Mary again fell silent for a minute or two, just staring out the window. Leah sat quietly on her lap, staring out the window with her. "Look!" Leah suddenly exclaimed. "The sky is turning all pink and purple. I never saw a sunrise before!"

"Is the sun rising already?" Mary spoke more as a statement than a question. "Soon others will be here. Then we'll go together to say goodbye for the last time. Can it really be the last time?" Her eyes sparkled, but not from tears. "Somehow I feel Lazarus is right. Something is different. Jesus did say he would come back. It's been three days." She spoke slowly, pausing, as if adding the lost pieces of a puzzle. Finding the last piece, she finished with excitement. "Somehow my soul sings within me a new song. God has done marvelous things. He has helped his servant Israel. I know he has."[14]

"Listen," said Leah. "It sounds like people running this way."

"The soldiers?" asked Cleopas, who had been silent most of the night, just taking in all that was said and done. He moved protectively closer to his wife, Martha. He had not wanted to be here. He would rather have been in his own home. It was Martha's desire to be here, and he loved her enough to do whatever he could for her. It was important for her to be with others who loved Jesus. And he had to admit, he learned a lot about their friend and his disciples and family. Now, however, he just wanted to go home where they would not be in so much danger.

"Quiet, everyone," cautioned Peter, a mixture of fear and authority in his voice. Moving toward the other window, he tried to see who was coming. He could see three figures running toward the house, but could not tell who they were. The room almost exploded with the inhaled breath and silent questions. No one moved. Everyone listened for the footsteps running toward the house.

With the coming of the dawn a new fear struck the hearts of the mourners. Would they, too, be arrested? Would the soldiers seek them out? Anxiously waiting for the unknown, they turned to face the door. Mary held the child close as they peered into the purple shadows.

Chapter Thirteen

He Is Not There!

"Look! There they are. It's not soldiers. It's some women and they are running this way," Leah said.

Mary moved closer to the window, still holding Leah close to her. "It looks like Mary Magdalene and Salome and someone else. I can't quite make out who the third person is. Quickly, someone open the door." Her voice quivered with excitement and expectation. "Let them in."

Peter, James and John all jumped at once to open the door. As John moved toward the door, Peter and James stepped aside and peered out the window behind Mary and Leah.

"Yes," said Peter. "It is Maggie and Salome and Mary, your mother, James." Peter had turned to Little James who was sometimes called James the Less to distinguish him from John's brother, James.

Little James ran to the door. "What is my mother doing out in the middle of the night?"

Leah looked up at Mary. "It's not the middle of the night anymore, is it?" she said innocently.

Mary smiled at her. "No, it's almost sunrise – a new day."

John opened the door and almost collided with Mary Magdalene, who was reaching to open the door from the outside. Her dark hair flying out from under her headdress fell around her shoulders as she suddenly stopped. Holding her hand against her chest, she took long, slow breaths before she could speak.

The other two women stopped short to keep from running into her. They also were puffing and breathing hard. Little James ran to his mother, full of concern. She looked pale and seemed to be having difficulty breathing.

"Mother! What in the world are you thinking about? You shouldn't be running through the streets of Jerusalem like a child. And at the crack of dawn yet! You're too old for that kind of stuff. Come and sit down. Let me get you some water."

While he was talking, James had his mother by the arm and leading her to a chair. He turned to go after the water, but Martha was already beside him, water in hand. Meanwhile, John helped Mary Magdalene to a chair and gave her some water while Peter looked after Salome.

The three women graciously accepted the water and took several deep breaths. Finally, able to make a sound, Mary spoke first to her son. "James stop fussing and pampering. I can take care of myself."

Mary was the oldest of the three women, but she was agile and had no trouble keeping up with the other two – well, not much trouble anyway. She was a petite, spunky widow who had lived alone since James left home. He was her baby. Much to the embarrassment of her children, she had refused to move in with any of them. Adult children were expected to care for their aging parents. James had scolded her, but to no avail. And now, here she was running through the streets of Jerusalem at dawn with two other women and no man to protect her. He was concerned, but she was making so much fuss that he knew she had to be all right. Throwing up his hands in mock despair, he grinned and backed away from her.

Salome, too, was breathing easier and gratefully thanked them for their concern. Salome was not much younger than Mary, but was taller and heavier. She didn't often run, so her lungs protested, crying for more oxygen. As her graying hair fell around her shoulders, Salome reached self-consciously to put it back in place. Then she straightened her shawl. "It was the most frightening and yet awesome sight I have ever seen!" she exclaimed in a hoarse whisper.

"What was? What are you talking about?" Peter asked. He probably spoke more impatiently than he intended. "Have you seen something? Heard something? What's happening?"

Salome glanced at Mary Magdalene, who was the chosen speaker for the group. Mary Magdalene became a part of their group, a trusted friend and worker with them, after Jesus healed her of demon possession. Because there were so many women with the name Mary and calling her Mary Magdalene seemed so long and formal, they fell into the habit of calling her Maggie. At first she was not sure she liked that, but the name sort of grew on her and it stuck.

"Yes," she said, nodding to Salome. "I'll tell you about it, but give us another minute or so to catch our breath." She took a swallow from the cup of cool water which John refilled for her.

After a moment of excited questions from everyone in the room, John raised his hands to get their attention. "Give them a minute. Let them begin at the beginning when they're ready. It's been a long night. A few more minutes won't hurt."

A hushed silence sparked with excited anticipation prevailed as Maggie finally began to speak. "He's not there! He said he would rise."[1] Her voice, which was normally a low, even-toned alto, sounded high-pitched and bouncy. Peter opened his mouth to interrupt with questions. Some glared at him, cautioning him not to interrupt. They wanted to hear what the women had to say, but too many questions had to be asked. Before Peter could form his, others began hurling their questions at her.

"What do you mean, he's not there? Who's not where? Risen? Where have you been so early in the morning?" The questions were coming so fast that she couldn't hear who was asking what and felt overwhelmed. She couldn't focus on any one question.

"Wait," she raised her voice, throwing up her hands over her ears. "I can't hear when you all talk at once." Silence fell over the room.

"She's right, of course," said John softly. "Begin at the beginning, Maggie. We'll listen. We're just impatient and anxious."

"And exhausted," added Andrew.

Maggie smiled and started again.

"Mary, Salome and I decided to go to the tomb before dawn. It was still dark. We didn't want to chance meeting the Roman soldiers and getting caught. We thought we would meet the rest of you there at daybreak. We could all pray our prayers of sorrow and maybe anoint our Lord since we couldn't do it earlier."

"Nicodemus and Joseph of Arimathea already anointed him before they put him in the tomb," Peter said. He had not quite grasped the full meaning of her earlier words. He could only concentrate on the facts before him. He couldn't yet comprehend the impossible.

"Oh," said Salome.

"We didn't know," added Mary.

"No," said Maggie, "we didn't know, and we knew you would be there, so we wanted to do what we could. We just needed to be there."

"We understand," said John. "We were just waiting for the dawn and we would have met you there to make it final."

"What about the stone? How did you think you would be able to move it? And even if you did, wouldn't there be an odor by now?" Thomas was serious, but turned abruptly when he heard laughter behind him. Lazarus couldn't help himself. Thomas, a little unnerved by the laughter, turned back to face the women. "What about the stone?" he asked again, dropping the remark about odor.

"We thought about that," answered Mary. "We had no idea how we would roll the stone away."

"Yes," said Salome, "even if we were not caught, we knew it would do us no good to be there with the stone in the way."

When Mary, the mother of Little James, got excited, she sparkled. Her whole body was in motion. She simply could not sit still. She jumped up and almost collided with Peter. Taking her empty cup, she moved toward the table to fill it, talking as she moved. "We were so scared we almost didn't go. We decided if we couldn't roll the stone away, we would wait for you. If you didn't show up, we would leave our spices and ointments outside beside the stone and then return to our homes. We thought somehow Jesus would know we tried."

Maggie added, "But when we got there, the stone was gone! It was lying on the ground a few feet away and the guards were nowhere to be seen."

Salome spoke excitedly, traces of fear still coloring her speech. "We were really frightened then, but we refused to turn back until we had found out what was going on."

"Did you go inside? The tomb, I mean." The women all turned, not expecting to hear a child's voice. Leah, who had grown progressively bolder as the night wore on, appeared not to notice their surprised looks. "Well, did you? Go inside, I mean," she asked again.

The three women turned and stared at the child on Mary's lap, seeing her for the first time. "Who is that?" Mary asked her son.

James smiled. "This is Leah. We've been telling stories all night. Leah's brother led the children in the waving of palm branches a week ago. We'll fill you in later."

Maggie, used to this group accepting the unusual, recovered from her shock of a child's presence. She nodded. "Yes, Leah, we went inside. We thought we may as well get started with what we were there to do. A young man dressed in a white robe was sitting there."

"An angel?" asked Leah. "You saw an angel?"

"Yes," answered Salome. "At least, we think he was an angel. None of us had ever seen one before, so we don't really know. I didn't believe it was possible to be more frightened than we had been as we walked those dark streets. But when we saw the angel, I knew what it meant to be paralyzed with fear. I couldn't move!"

"Nor could I," said Mary. "For a minute, I thought maybe we were in the wrong place."

Little James looked at his mother with a sly grin on his face. "Why, Mother! I'm surprised! I didn't think you were afraid of anything."

Mary glared at her son. "Have you ever seen an angel?" she asked, still glaring at him.

"No," he admitted.

"Then keep your smart remarks to yourself," she said.

"Yes, Mother." Little James said with mock meekness. He couldn't keep from laughing at the seriousness of his mother's voice. He knew she wasn't really angry with him. James was not only her baby, but he was also the youngest of the disciples. He often seemed no more than a youth.

Maggie, who was used to the gentle banter between mother and son, smiled at them and continued the account of the morning. "I was sure it was the right place. I thought possibly the man in white was one of the guards, although it was strange dress for a guard. Then we thought maybe the guards had moved Jesus. Talk about fear; I was beginning to tremble. I think Mary and Salome were, too."

"Yes," said Salome, her voice still trembling. "I just knew we were all going to be arrested – or worse."

Maggie picked up the story again. "We saw the empty stone shelf where the body of Jesus should have been lying, and the man in the white sitting there as if he belonged. Looking from one to the other, none of us needed to say a word. We each knew exactly what the other was thinking. We had to get out of there – and fast. We started backing slowly from the tomb, hoping to be able to run before we were caught. The man spoke and the sound of his voice was so...so different. I'm not sure I can really describe it."

"Sort of like golden bells," said James' mother.

"Or the ripple of a rushing stream," added Salome.

"Yes," said Mary, the mother of Jesus. "That's it. Although it has been over thirty years since I heard the angel speak, I remember the sound very well."

Maggie turned her thoughts and her words back to the angel in the tomb. "He asked why we were there and who we were looking for. 'Why would you look for the living among the dead? He's not here. He has risen!'"

James' mother added with a nervous little laugh, "Then he told us not to stand there with our mouths open, but to go and tell Peter and the rest of you what we saw."

"And you let that go without question?" James was smiling at his mother. She tried unsuccessfully to glare at him as Salome spoke.

"Well, we didn't need to be told a second time to go," Salome said with a nervous giggle. "We turned and ran as fast as we could to do what he told us to do – that is, tell you what we heard and saw."

"Jesus did tell us he would be raised from the dead in three days."

Maggie's voice was losing some of the terrified excitement and was beginning to sound more perplexed and pained. "But where is he? We know the tomb is empty, but we don't know where he is."

A deep, penetrating silence hung in the air as the little group of friends tried to absorb what the women had told them. Suddenly, the full impact of her words hit him, and Peter jumped to his feet. "I'm going to go see," he exclaimed. And he was out the door before anyone could stop him.

"I'll go, too," said John and he followed on the heels of Peter. Being younger, he soon caught up with Peter and even passed him. The others crowded around the door and windows to watch the two running figures until they could no longer be seen.

Leah jumped from Mary's lap. She was already at the door on her way out to run after Peter and John when Adam grabbed her.

"Oh no, you don't," he said. "You might get away with asking questions and making a nuisance of yourself here, but we're not going to turn you loose on an unsuspecting city."

"But I want to go see the angel," she cried.

"Some other time, little sister," said Adam. "For now, we'll let Peter and John take care of it. They don't need you under foot."

Adam picked Leah up and carried her back to their parents. They, too, had jumped when they saw her head for the door. Leah's dark eyes were spilling over with tears as Adam set her down beside her mother.

"I wanted to see the angel," she cried. "I wasn't going to get in the way. I just wanted to go see."

"Leah!" Her father spoke a little sharply. Even though she had seemed older than her six and a half years most of the night, the tiredness caught up with her and she was now very much the child, not an adult. She stopped sobbing, but tears continued to roll down her cheeks as she turned toward her father.

"Come here," he said. And she got up without delay. When she got close to him, he gathered her in his arms and put her on his lap. He held her, speaking softly so only she could hear until he realized she was asleep. Lovingly he brushed her hair from her face. It had been a long night for all of them – and especially for one so young. He shook his head sadly as he glanced from his sleeping daughter to his son, who sat with his face dropped in his hands. He couldn't keep a small tear from trickling down his own face as he thought of the changes in his family.

Time ticked by very slowly as they waited for Peter and John to return. The three women who had been at the tomb waited with the rest, softly talking among themselves. It was all so incredible, they would be glad for confirmation of their story. They appreciated a time of quiet to reflect and review in their minds. Thomas kept watch by the door, going out occasionally to see if Peter and John were returning.

The others huddled here and there talking in hushed tones as the morning sun continued to climb higher in the sky. They waited in fear, pondering the night's activities and the morning's news. Peter and John would soon return and give credence to the story they all wanted to believe but found so incredible.

Finally, when he could stand the suspense no longer, Thomas said, "I'm going to find them. They've been gone too long."

"I'll go with you," said Andrew, as he got up and moved toward the door with Thomas.

Before they reached the door, however, they heard Peter and John returning, the sound of their feet echoing through the alley as their sandals slapped against the cobblestones. James opened the door at the same time Peter was reaching for it. All around the room excited and hopeful eyes watched.

"Well?" asked James. "What did you find? Was he there? Is the tomb empty?"

John, breathing hard, slapped his brother on the back. "It's true!" he exclaimed. "It's true! The women are right – not that we didn't believe them," he added. "The stone is indeed rolled away from the opening. There are no guards. The place is empty."

"Did you see the angel?" asked Leah. The new wave of excitement and noise had awakened her.

"No," said John, "there was no angel, only the grave clothes and

194

an empty tomb."

"Oh," said Leah with a note of disappointment in her voice. Her father pulled her closer to him. She was still sleepy and tired, but she wouldn't allow herself to miss anything.

"Here, John, sit down before you fall down," said James, pulling a chair out for his brother. "Someone take care of Peter. He looks like death itself."

"And you complained about us running through the city!" exclaimed Salome as she handed Peter a cup of water. He just glared, his breath coming too hard for him to respond.

"So, tell us what you found," said Thomas, anxious to know the truth. "We were just getting ready to come looking for you. If you didn't see an angel, what did you see?"

Peter sat still for what seemed a long time, and John waited for him to speak first. When his breathing had settled back to almost normal, he said, "John got there before I did, but he didn't go inside. He was leaning over, looking inside, waiting for me so we could go in together in case the guards were hiding inside to ambush us. I stepped around him and entered the tomb. No one was there. No guards. No angels. No Jesus. The grave clothes were there, but there was no body."

All around the room questions were flying like birds in the morning hunting for food. Finally, Maggie asked the question they were all thinking, but were afraid to ask. "But where is he, Peter? Where is the body? Jesus said he would rise, but what does that mean and where is he?" No one could give her an answer, not even Lazarus.

Then everyone was speaking at once again, trying to make sense of all the strange happenings. In the midst of all the excited chatter that followed, no one noticed Maggie slip quietly out the door – no one, that is, except Leah, who sensed that she wanted to be alone. Leah said nothing.

After a while someone said, "Maggie, tell us again about the angel in the tomb. Maybe you missed something." There was no answer. In the silence everyone looked from one to another.

"Maggie? Where is she? Where did she go?" It was uncertain who really asked the questions.

"She went out," said Leah matter-of-factly.

"What do you mean, 'She went out'?" asked Peter, sounding a little irritable. "Where did she go? And when?"

"I don't know where she went," answered Leah, "but she just went out the door while you folks were all chattering."

"Leah!" Her mother reached to draw her daughter into the corner away from the activity.

Peter had to laugh in spite of himself. "Did she say anything?"

"No," said Leah. "She just looked sort of sad. I kind of thought she wanted to be by herself for a while."

"You're probably right, Leah," said John. "We've all been so caught up in our own grief, and then the excitement of the strange news, that we failed to notice some things. Maybe I should go find her." He turned toward the door.

Chapter Fourteen

I Have Seen Him!

Thinking perhaps Mary Magdalene returned to the tomb, John started to go find her. Before he laid a hand on the door, however, Maggie opened it and stood in the door way for a minute with an odd sort of glow to her face.

"There you are, Maggie. Where have you been? We were beginning to worry about you. John was just going to search for you." Salome ran to her friend and embraced her. She often spoke rapidly, running her sentences together when she was excited.

"I'm sorry," said Maggie. "I didn't mean to alarm anyone. I just needed to walk and think. I didn't really have any destination in mind, but before I even thought about it, I was back at the tomb. It really is empty. And I..."

Salome rushed on interrupting her, "Are you all right? You look..." She searched for a word to describe her friend, but settled for "...Different."

"I saw him," Mary Magdalene spoke so softly her voice was just above a whisper. "I saw Jesus."[1] It took several seconds for her words to register before questions began to fly.

"What? Where? When?"

"Tell us, Maggie," said Peter.

"I slipped out while you were all talking. I only intended to walk for a few minutes. I guess it's been longer," she began softly. "When I found myself at the tomb, I wasn't afraid anymore – not of the guards, or of the angel." Maggie laughed at her own attempt to deny her fear. "At least, that's what I tried to tell myself. Since I was there anyway, I thought I would just look inside the empty tomb once more. Nothing changed. No one was there – not even the angel." She glanced at Leah, who grinned. "I just stood there for a while, thinking and trying to make sense of it all."

Mary Magdalene paused, embarrassed, as she struggled with how much of her feelings to share with her friends. Swallowing hard, she pushed on with words she found easy to voice, and at the same time difficult – easy because they seemed to flow without effort of thought and difficult because of the emotion which propelled them.

"The tears kept spilling over my eyes and down my face." She tried a small laugh. Her hands went to her face. "I probably look pretty awful." She didn't wait for an answer, not really expecting them to agree or disagree with her. "The memories kept coming in torrents almost as if the tears were pulling them from some place deep inside my soul, memories I thought were long forgotten."

Sensing another story to add to their memories of Jesus, John pulled a chair toward her. "Come, sit here, Maggie. Let me get you something to drink and maybe a bite to eat."

"Thank you, John." She smiled as she gratefully accepted both the chair and the refreshment.

Maggie stared into the flickering candlelight which was no longer needed since the sun was shining brightly. In all the excitement no one had thought to extinguish it. She struggled, trying to block out the painful past while at the same time remembering every detail. Softly, almost urgently, she pressed on with her story to a silent, listening group of friends.

"As I stood there looking at that empty tomb, I remembered how seven demons once possessed my mind and body. I used to just live from day to day not knowing where my life was headed. With every rising sun I hoped my mind and body would cooperate and let me live a normal life – at least for that one day. Many days I really didn't care if I lived or died. More often than not I preferred to die, except I always lacked the courage to do anything about it. That old feeling of depression and gloom were beginning to settle over me again as I stood there in front of that gaping place of burial. Then I remembered the day Jesus walked into my life."

Once again she was conscious of the tears flowing down her cheeks, tears that seemed to have a mind of their own, flowing at will. Before her brother or parents could stop her, Leah jumped down and ran to Maggie's side, offering her a small piece of cloth. She put her arms around the woman's neck. "I'm glad Jesus found you," she whispered with an innocent truthfulness.

Maggie smiled through her tears, offering her lap for Leah. The little girl was glad to take it. She wanted to hear the story Maggie was telling. Not sure who this charming little girl was, Maggie somehow felt better having the child with her. Giving Leah a gentle squeeze, she hurried on.

"When I first saw Jesus, I wondered what kind of man he was. Some people said he was a carpenter from Nazareth. I wondered how a carpenter could do all the things people said he did and was doing. He didn't look very strong or powerful from a distance.

"The closer he came to me, the more I felt my body begin to signal the beginning of those terrible bouts of demon-possession. I just knew I would to do something dumb or strange or embarrassing. I looked for a place to run and hide, but his eyes met mine and I became like a stone – or a tree. My feet felt as if they had grown roots. He stopped in front of me. Without saying a word he held out his hand to me. I placed my hand in his. Tears began to flow. The strangeness was gone forever.[2] I don't know how he did it. I only knew the demons left me and no longer controlled my body and mind. I loved Jesus from the bottom of my heart with a love that only could be from God. I would have gone to the ends of the earth for him, as I know all of you would have. And yet, there I was at that empty tomb and couldn't even find his body to weep over.

"I remembered the past, and the reality of the present became more fearful. I wanted to go back inside and couldn't move. As I clung to the side of the tomb for support, grief consumed me and I wept once more. Finally, that wave of grief receded and I thought maybe I could look inside once again. I stooped to go in, and this time I saw two angels!" She smiled at Leah, expecting her comment this time.

"Two angels?" asked Leah. "When Peter and John were there, there weren't any angels. I bet they just like to talk to women." Leah was so matter-of-fact and positive that they all had to laugh, breaking the seriousness of the mood a little.

"Don't forget an angel appeared to Joseph – twice." Her brother had to tease her a little.

"Oh, that's right," she answered. Then she looked up into Maggie's moist eyes with her big, round ones. "Did they talk to you?" she asked.

"Yes, they asked me why I was crying." Maggie stopped, afraid that what she was about to say would sound so impossible that no one would believe her.

"Go on," encouraged Salome. "We want to hear everything."

Mary Magdalene continued cautiously. "I heard a sound behind me and I turned. Through the blur of tears in my eyes, I assumed the man I saw was the gardener. He also asked me why I was crying and who I was looking for. The voice was familiar, but I couldn't let my mind hear what my heart was saying." Maggie looked a little embarrassed.

"Somehow I managed to control the sound of my voice. At least, I think I did. I told him I was looking for the body of Jesus, who had been put in that tomb but was now missing. I asked him if he knew where they took the body, thinking maybe he had put Jesus someplace else. The man smiled at me. And then..." Maggie's face became radiant. "Then he spoke my name. For a split second I think my heart stopped beating. I thought I must be dreaming. Maybe the demons were back... playing tricks with my mind."

Maggie glanced at Mary, the mother of Jesus, who was smiling broadly at her, and nodded. She didn't know how it was possible, but somehow Maggie knew his mother already understood the truth in her heart.

Maggie continued, "I said, 'Teacher? Master?' I lifted my face for the first time in our conversation. Our eyes met and I knew. I fell at his feet, but he wouldn't let me touch him. I was so overjoyed and yet so pained. I wanted so much to touch him, to know he was real and not just my imagination. I wanted to believe everything would be the same as before, even while my heart told me that could never be.

"'Don't hold on to me,' he said. 'I haven't ascended to my Father yet.'"

All around the room, the sound of gasps could be heard followed by the murmuring of questions. "He is really alive? You have seen him? I knew it was true, but..." Jesus' mother, who had been silently considering all that was being told to them, could no longer contain her excitement and joy. Tears were flowing from her eyes as they were from Maggie's.

"Yes, Mary," Maggie declared softly. "He is really alive! I have seen him and have talked to him. I thought I could never love him more than I did that day he cleansed me and made me whole, but seeing him in that garden, I knew my life was changing again. Isn't it strange in a wonderful sort of way that every time we meet Jesus our lives become different? He is indeed alive. And because he lives, we, too, shall live – truly live."

"I told you God always does that," remarked Leah.

"Does what, Leah?" asked Maggie.

"God always does what we don't expect him to do, 'cause he likes to see us happy."

"You're certainly right there," laughed Maggie. "Just being there with him, knowing he is alive, I was so happy I wanted to stay in that garden with him. I wanted to hear his plans and his goals for my life. I just wanted to sit at his feet and hear all the stories he had to tell. Especially, I wanted to hear about those three days in the grave. But he said he must go. I had to be content knowing that he had been there and that I would see him again.

"I came back to tell you. Soon we'll have to leave this place and the comfort of our fellowship together. We must follow him."

* * *

News of the empty tomb filled them with new hope and excitement. Mary Magdalene's news of having actually seen and talked with the Lord gave them new food for thought. Thoughts of dispersing and going their separate ways were put on hold. Their original plan was to go together to the tomb for a final farewell. Maggie's news changed that. How do you say goodbye to someone who has returned? Plans needed to be changed, but how? What should they do now? Thoughts of sleep were forgotten as discussion persisted the rest of the day. The once grief-stricken, mourners were charged with excitement.

Finally as the day was nearing its close, Mary Magdalene and Martha began automatically to fuss around, gathering dirty dishes, picking up a little here and a little there, anything to keep busy. Others began to gather their things to leave. Cleopas convinced his wife they should leave. Sadly they prepared to return to their home in Emmaus. They said goodbye, thanked John for his hospitality, and promised to get together again soon. It was seven miles or so to Emmaus. They would have to hurry to get home before dark.

Thomas also left. He needed to take a walk "to clear the cobwebs," he said. So much had happened. He had to have some time to sort out his thoughts and sift through all his doubts.

Later, the ones who were left began to make their plans for returning to their homes as well. They were sharing thoughts and ideas when a figure of a man suddenly stood before them.[3] They sat with eyes wide and mouths open, afraid to speak. Yet there was a feeling of growing unity and a spirit of love among them.

"It's Jesus!" cried Leah as she ran to him. Jesus smiled at her and took her in his arms. Then he spoke to the people. "Peace."

His mother hesitated, then ran to him. Holding Leah in one arm, he put the other around her, assuring her that he was all right. The others crowded around, wanting to touch him. He then kissed his mother, set the child down, and he was gone. As quickly and mysteriously as he had come, he was gone.

But they knew. Christ the Lord is indeed alive forever more! He is alive!

Epilogue

The Road Home

"Hurry, Martha! The sun is almost gone and we dare not be out on the road when the darkness prevails. Robbers may be lying in wait – not that we have anything of value for them to take except our lives. I guess if a robber wants to strike, he will do it whether we have valuables or not. After all the strange events of the last few days, who knows what might happen next? We must hurry. It's not much farther. God will guide us."

"I'm hurrying as fast as I can, Cleopas," Martha cried, choking back a sob. "I'm so tired. We've walked almost seven miles. We should've stayed in Jerusalem until morning."[1]

Cleopas was a small man, and like others of his age, he sported a well-trimmed beard. He walked with a limp because of a childhood accident. Between his pain and Martha's childless status, their grief was great until the day Jesus came to Emmaus. Jesus didn't heal their bodies; however, they no longer grieved old losses or held on to resentments of the past or present. Jesus loved them just the way they were, and that was all that mattered.

Martha stumbled again, and Cleopas gently placed one arm around her waist and held her hand in his other hand. He felt a little guilty about insisting on leaving when they did, but he wanted desperately to be in his own home where life was stable and predictable.

"We're almost home," he said. "It's been difficult for both of us. It was harder for his mother and closer friends. It's still hard to believe that just last week he was alive and well. If only he had listened to his disciples. If only he had stayed away from Jerusalem."

"Yes, if only. Oh, Cleopas, do you suppose there could be any truth to the rumors, the stories?" Martha's voice sounded weary, but a tiny spark of hope prevailed. "Surely Mary Magdalene wouldn't have made up that story about the garden. If Jesus is not – you know – dead, what do you think happened to his body?" Martha began to shiver, not from cold, but more from the excitement of all the possibilities.

"Are you cold, Martha? Here, take my cloak." Cleopas removed his outer coat of gray cloth and placed it around her shoulders. As he was adjusting it so it would not slip off, he noticed a shadow of a man beside them. In the darkness of the twilight and in his fright at seeing a stranger, Cleopas drew Martha closer to him and would have run, except the stranger spoke. His voice was soft and didn't sound threatening like a robber would have sounded. As a matter of fact, it sounded strangely familiar.

"What are you talking about?" the stranger asked them. "You seem to have lost a good friend. Who was he? Would I know him?"

The stranger began to walk beside them as they continued on their way. Martha and Cleopas looked at each other and then at the stranger. Cleopas thought, *He looks familiar, but I just can't seem to place him. I wonder if Martha feels it too.*

Martha did feel a strange warming sensation similar to what she had known only in close friendships. She wondered, *How can that be? The stranger is a friendly person, but should we trust him? And yet there's something about him that invites trust. I wonder if Cleopas feels it too.* Martha kept her thoughts to herself, watching with interest to see what Cleopas would to do.

Cleopas looked at the stranger with wonder. "Are you the only person in Jerusalem who doesn't know what's been happening?" he asked. "It's been a very strange and sorrowful few days."

"What things have happened?" asked the stranger.

Cleopas couldn't believe that anyone wouldn't know all the events of the past week. He thought, *Maybe the man has been away. Should I tell him? Should I ignore him and just get Martha to hurry a little more?*

Cleopas struggled with his thoughts. Finally, deciding to trust the stranger, Cleopas began to tell him about the past three days. "We were speaking of our friend, Jesus of Nazareth," Cleopas said. "He was a prophet, you know. No one ever spoke the way he did. He spoke with authority and truth before God and all people. Our chief priests delivered him up to be condemned to death." His voice broke and he took a minute to regain his composure.

Martha entered her thoughts on the story when Cleopas stopped. Choking back her own tears, she said, "Yes, and they...they crucified him. We hoped he was the Messiah, the one who would redeem Israel, but when I saw him on that cross, it was as if the world had ended. Even then he still talked and acted like the Christ, he died." Her voice fell to barely a whisper.

Cleopas regained his composure and picked up where Martha stopped. "That's right. Jesus died. We saw it. We saw them take him from the cross. Joseph of Arimetha and Nicodemus, friends from the Sanhedrin, put him in a tomb. That was three days ago – three long, weary days."

"But that's not all," Martha broke in excitedly. "Some women in our group went to the tomb early this morning, and the body was gone! It has disappeared! And they said they had seen a vision of angels who told them he was alive!"

"Martha, don't get carried away," Cleopas warned. "Remember how our friends sometimes exaggerate and tell sensational stories."

"They wouldn't deliberately lie about it." Martha stiffened, and with an edge to her voice said, "Remember Peter and John went to see for themselves. The tomb is empty."

"I know," said Cleopas, "but we can't jump to conclusions. After all, we were up all night. And if we don't get home and get some sleep, we'll be seeing more than angels and visions."

The stranger spoke again. His voice was firm but soft, speaking with an authority of knowledge. "How foolishly you talk! You are so slow to believe all that the prophets have said. Didn't they say it would be necessary for the Christ to suffer before entering his glory?"

"Yes, but..."

The stranger continued to explain the Scriptures to them as they walked on their way. He began with Moses and the prophets and taught them until they reached their home. As Martha and Cleopas turned to go into their house, the stranger turned to continue on his way.

Cleopas spoke, "It's very late. It could be dangerous for anyone to journey alone. Stay the night with us. Tell us more of the Scriptures. Teach us more about the Christ. You seem to know so much more than we, who have known him for such a short time."

"Thank you," he said. "May God bless you for your hospitality."

"Yes, come and join us for a quick meal. I will fix us some cheese and bread, and I think I have some figs and dates. Please make yourself comfortable."

The stranger entered the gate to their house with them. Cleopas sat with him in the darkness of the garden talking and sharing stories. Martha, tired as she was, suddenly felt full of energy, and she quickly set about to prepare a modest meal. Although they were not poor, Cleopas and Martha preferred not to have servants. When she had finished preparing the meal, she called, "Cleopas, bring our guest to the table. The food is prepared."

Cleopas and the stranger rose together and walked toward the door where the warmth of candlelight spilled out to invite them into the room. Inside the door Martha had placed a basin of water, a towel and a small stool.

"Sit down, my friend," said Cleopas motioning to the stool. "Let me wash the dust of the day from your feet."

The stranger sat down, and Cleopas removed his sandals. He cupped the water in his hands and poured water over the stranger's feet, wondering about the strange scars on them. He dried them with the towel Martha left for them. Cleopas then washed his own feet, and they moved to the table which was waiting for them. The stranger in the light of the lamp looked very familiar, almost like their beloved teacher. But no, that was too absurd. That was impossible!

Even though the custom was for men to eat first and women to wait until later, Martha and Cleopas always ate together. This night was no different. The stranger didn't seem to mind her presence. He even seemed to enjoy her remarks as they sat together, eating the simple meal and enjoying more teaching of the Scriptures as well as simple conversation.

"Have some more of Martha's delicious bread," said Cleopas as he handed a loaf to the stranger. They still didn't know his name, but were content to wait until he was ready to reveal it. The man took the bread from Cleopas and smiled with a radiance they could not understand. He lifted the bread with both hands and holding it at eye level said, "Father, bless this bread as you have blessed all bread. May this be a reminder to your children of your love." Then he broke the bread and, his eyes burning into their very souls, he offered it to them. Remembrance of the description the disciples had given of that last meal at Passover dawned upon them. With his eyes searching theirs, tears of recognition and shame of not having realized who he was began to flow. Martha and Cleopas reached to embrace him. He smiled again at them and was gone!

Martha and Cleopas turned to each other, tears in their eyes sparkling in the lamplight. Excitement was building. "We should have known. We should have known! Didn't we feel a warm feeling as he walked with us?" Martha began to bubble with excitement. "Didn't we sense something different about him?"

"Yes, and I kept thinking how much he looked like our Lord. But I just wouldn't let my heart believe it. We must go back to Jerusalem in the morning to let the rest know." Cleopas was as excited as Martha. He could hardly talk without laughing and crying at the same time.

Cleopas and Martha looked at each other, their eyes still glistening with tears and excitement. Together, almost as one, they said, "No. We must return tonight. We must go now."

Martha didn't take time to even clear the table. Although it would be past midnight when they arrived, they hurried back to Jerusalem, where they found most of the others still in John's house. They told their story and heard how Jesus had appeared behind the locked doors earlier the evening before.

It was incredible, but it was true! The Lord has risen. The Lord has risen indeed!

NOTES AND REFERENCES

Prologue

1. Matthew 26:17-30, Mark 14:17-26, Luke 22:1-39, John 13:1, 18:1

– Each of the four gospels incorporate this in their account of the last days of Jesus. John is the only one who speaks of the foot washing in Chapter 13.

2. Matthew 26:36-46, Mark 14:32-42, Luke 22:39-46

The three synoptic gospels give the account of Jesus praying in the garden. (Synoptic means similar. The first three gospels are similar in their recording of the life of Jesus.) John skips over it and goes immediately to the betrayal by Judas.

3. Matthew 26:47-56, Mark 14:43-50, Luke 22:47-53, John 18:2-11

4. Matthew 26:69-75, Mark 14:66-72, Luke 22:54-62, John 18:15-18, 25-27.

Peter wants to know what is happening, but is afraid. He follows at a distance hoping not to be seen and recognized.

Chapter One

1. John 19:25-27

John is the only gospel who makes mention of the compassionate gift of Jesus for his mother and his friend.

2. Matthew 27:57-61, Mark 15:42-46, Luke 23:50-56, John 19:38-42

The synoptic gospels tell about Joseph of Arimathea coming to claim the body of Jesus. Only John mentions Nicodemus being there.

Chapter Two
  1. John 19:30
  2. John 19:38-41

Chapter Three
  1. Matthew 3:1-17, Mark 1:1-8, Luke 3:1-20, John 1:19-34

The story of John the Baptist is recorded in all the gospels. Each one tells it a little differently. Luke gives us the most information, including the reasons for John's imprisonment and death.

Chapter Four
  1. Matthew 3:16-17, Mark 1:10-11, Luke 3:21-22, John 1:32, 12:28

All the gospels tell of the spirit descending on Jesus at his Baptism. However, only the synoptic gospels tell of the voice. Matthew says, "This is my beloved . . ." The other two say, "You are . . ." John records the voice at a different time and then not the same as the others.
  2. Matthew 4:1-11, Mark 1:12-13, Luke 4:1-13

Matthew and Luke both give longer accounts of the temptations. Mark only says Jesus was tempted. John does not mention them at all.
  3. Isaiah 11:6

Many times children are more perceptive than adults – especially when the adult is lost in the throes of grief.
  4. Deuteronomy 8:3

The Old Testament was the source and background of much of the teaching of the New Testament.
  5. Deuteronomy 6:16
  6. Deuteronomy 6:13

Chapter Five
  1. Zachariah 13:7, Isaiah 40:11, 53:6-7
  The prophets often referred to the coming Messiah as a shepherd of the flock.
  2. Matthew 16:21-13, Mark 8:31-33

Chapter Six
  1. John 3:1-21
  John is the only gospel who tells the story of Nicodemus coming to Jesus seeking truth.
  2. John 1:45-49
  Again, John is the only gospel to record the encounter with Nathaniel.
  3. Ezekiel 11:19
  4. Genesis 22:17
  5. John 7:45-52
  6. John 19:38-42

Chapter Seven
  1. John 4:4-43
  John is the only gospel to tell the story of the woman at the well.
  2. John 8:7

Chapter Eight
  1. Matthew 9:27-31, Mark 8:22-26, Luke 18:35-43, John 9:140
  All of the gospels record events of healing of the blind. John and Luke give more details – John more than Luke. Joshua is a composite of blind beggars who were healed. It was the belief of the day that a person born blind was the result of sin.

Chapter Nine

    1. Luke 2:41-50

Luke is the only gospel who records anything concerning the childhood of Jesus and even he limits his account to this brief passage.

    2. Matthew 3:11-12, Mark 1:1-8, Luke 3:4-16, John 1:29-34

    3. Luke 10:38-41

While John tells us a lot about Mary and Martha, sisters of Lazarus, Luke is the only one who records this incident.

    4. John 11:1-44

John is the only one who gives us the account of Lazarus' death and resurrection. Some authorities say the Jews believed the soul didn't leave the body until three days after death. Therefore, Jesus waited until the fourth day so there would be no doubt about him bringing Lazarus back from death.

Chapter Ten

    1. Matthew 19:13-14, Mark 10:13-16, Luke 18:15-17

Jesus always had time for the "left out" of society – whether lepers or children. They were all important to him.

    2. Genesis 22:17

    3. Matthew 14:15-21, Mark 6:34-44, Luke 9:10-17, John 5:5-14

    4. Matthew 14:22-23, Mark 6:45-51, John, 6:16-21

    5. Matthew 21:1-9, Mark 11:1-10, Luke 19:29-38, John 12:12-15

    6. Luke 19:41-42

    7. Luke 23:36

    8. John 19:30

Chapter Eleven
1. Matthew 4:18-22, Mark 1:16-20, John 1:35-42
2. Exodus 20 – The Ten Commandments or the Decalogue
3. John 13:3-14
4. Matthew 26:33-35, Mark 14:29-31, Luke 22:33-34, John 13:37-38
5. Isaiah 6:1-8

Chapter Twelve
1. Luke 1:26-38
Luke is the only one to give the account of the annunciation of Mary.
2. Luke 1:36-56
3. Matthew 1:18-25
4. Matthew 2:1, Luke 2:1-7
5. Luke 2:8-21
6. Matthew 2:1-12
7. Matthew 2:16-21
8. Matthew 2:22-23
9. John 2:1-11
10. Matthew 12:46-50, Mark 3:31-35, Luke 8:19-21
11. Luke 23:34
12. John 19:26
13. John 19:27
14. Luke 1:46-55

Chapter Thirteen
1. Matthew 28:1-7, Mark 16:1-10, Luke 24: 1-12, John 20:1-18

Chapter Fourteen
1. John 20:11-18
2. Luke 8:2
3. John 20:19-29

Epilogue
1. Luke 24:13-35